D1131023

Counseling

in the

Elementary

School

Counseling in the Elementary School

WILLIAM H. VAN HOOSE
Wayne State University

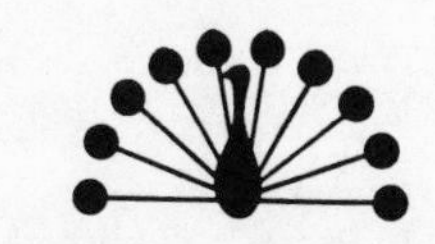

F. E. PEACOCK PUBLISHERS, INC.
ITASCA, ILLINOIS

Printed in the U.S.A.
Library of Congress Catalog Card Number 68-26697

To
Freddie and Pamela

Preface

WITHIN THE PAST FEW YEARS educators, social scientists, and the general public have given increased attention to the elementary school. Numerous societal changes leading to increased demands and pressures upon schools, teachers, and most importantly upon children, make it obvious that some new approaches to helping children are necessary. New understandings in the psychology of human development have heightened our awareness of the need to do as much as possible to aid pupils during their formative years.

The emergence of guidance in grades K–6 is a development that holds much promise for helping children succeed in the educational endeavor. Counselors have been selected and employed to assist children directly and indirectly in making the most of school and life experiences. These specialists contribute to the total development of children through three processes: counseling, consulting, and coordinating. All of these functions are important; however, counseling is the key guidance function and contributes more directly to the realization of guidance goals than either of the other functions.

This book represents an effort to provide focus and direction to the field of elementary school counseling. The developmental approach is emphasized. The book is based on the belief that counseling is concerned with all children in all aspects of development—cognitive, emotional, and vocational. Counseling is viewed as a professional task performed by professionally competent personnel. The counselor is a school staff member, a colleague of teachers, and a special helper for students.

Counseling in the Elementary School describes the *content* as well as the *process* of counseling. The book presents a concise and coherent description of developmental processes organized around the concept of developmental tasks and life stages. Several implications for counseling are drawn from this material and from chapters dealing with behavior, societal influences, and learning.

While this book is geared primarily to the needs of counselors, counselor educators, and graduate students in guidance, much of the material is relevant to all educators and to other professionals who work with children and youth. Teachers, administrators, and other pupil personnel specialists will find the chapters on behavior, child study, and consultation particularly helpful.

The author is grateful to several individuals who assisted in the preparation of this manuscript. To my secretary, Mrs. Vivian Dennis, who typed the entire manuscript, I am most grateful. Dr. Nancy Schlossberg, my colleague and friend, read several chapters and provided many helpful suggestions. I am especially grateful to Dr. Herman J. Peters for his perceptive comments and his generous encouragement. Finally, I am most grateful to my wife Hazel, for her patience and understanding throughout the writing of this book.

William H. Van Hoose

Plymouth, Michigan
February, 1968

Contents

PART I

Perspective

THE PURPOSE OF PART I is to provide an overview of guidance and counseling in the elementary school. Some understanding of the development of guidance and counseling at the elementary level will enable the reader to gain greater familiarity with the present character of guidance and counseling for elementary school children.

Guidance is described as an integral part of the educational program which emphasizes total development of all students. Counseling is viewed as the key guidance activity. Several conditions which create a need for organized guidance and counseling for all children are described. This perspective also highlights some of the differences between elementary and secondary school counseling. A short statement of the author's viewpoint is found at the end of Chapter 1.

Chapter 1

Counseling in the Elementary School: Perspective

GUIDANCE IN THE SCHOOL SETTING represents an attempt to help pupils develop to the maximum of their potential, both as individuals and as learners. Guidance is specialized assistance for all children and youth: the normal, the malfunctioning, the bright, and the dull. Guidance gives full consideration to the total development of each individual. Thus, the guidance function focuses upon cognitive, social, and vocational development as well as upon self-understanding and self-direction. Guidance and counseling require the services of professionally competent personnel. Adequate training at the graduate school level, appropriate experiences with children and youth, and proper personal characteristics, are all basic requirements for the school counselor.

The guidance activity and the instructional activity are interdependent and reciprocal. Learning becomes more meaningful as children acquire an understanding of their capacities and interests through counseling. The counselor is a co-worker of the teacher in assisting children to implement plans made through guidance activities.

To emphasize the above points, we paraphrase Miller who writes that guidance is an integral part of the educational program and is based upon the democratic concept of the dignity and worth of the individual. Developing in the American culture, guidance in secondary schools and personnel work in higher education place major emphasis upon assisting the individual to develop toward his own best self-realization.[1] Similar objectives underlie the development and expansion of guidance and counseling services in the elementary schools.

Need for Guidance

Several societal conditions and conditions within the school itself contribute to the need for guidance services beginning in the elementary grades. Several factors which suggest that guidance will become increasingly important at all levels of education are discussed in Part II of this book. As a reference point for what is to follow however, it is appropriate to identify some of the general conditions which contribute to the need for guidance and counseling in schools.

Peters writes that the first condition which reveals a need for guidance is the concern of youth itself for direction. Children and youth of today are growing up in an age of complexity and uncertainty. The best approach to helping children and youth understand who they are and what they are capable of becoming is through an organized program of guidance. Peters stresses the importance of viewing guidance not only from the perspective of cultural conditions, but also from the vantage point of school concerns. One of the major concerns is academic success. This alone is of sufficient magnitude to justify guidance at all levels of education.[2]

More recently Downing has identified several conditions which suggest that guidance is more important now than ever before. Among the conditions listed are the following:

1. The psychological aspects of pupil development are receiving more attention. A better understanding of children is being realized as a more intensive and comprehensive study of all aspects of development is made.
2. Problems occur as concomitants to growth and development. The need for providing assistance with these problems, if good adjustment is to be realized, is apparent. Physical growth takes place at a rapid rate, and new insights are needed for a

[1] Carroll H. Miller, *Guidance Services* (New York: Harper & Row, Publishers, 1965), pp. 7–8.

[2] Herman J. Peters, "The Nature of the Guidance Function," *Counselor Education and Supervision,* Vol. 3, No. 3 (Spring, 1964), pp. 122–28.

valid understanding of these physical changes. Wholesome attitudes toward the whole process of development are needed as learning occurs and understandings increase through instruction and guidance activities. Mental development proceeds at a rapid pace during childhood. The implications are obvious: there is a need to provide an educational environment conducive to maximum development with appropriate challenges and some assurance of successful accomplishments.

3. The teachers' major responsibility is instruction: this leaves little time or energy for assisting youngsters with problems unrelated to instructional activities. Problems of social adjustment and personality reorientation require the services of a competent counselor. . . .[3]

There is considerable evidence to support the conclusion that much more help is needed by children in their formative years than is presently being provided. Recent research has concluded that potential school dropouts and potential delinquents can be identified during the elementary school years. Further, the evidence suggests that such problems could often be prevented through a broader program of school services and activities.

The impact of childhood experiences upon later functioning is illustrated in the Kagan and Moss report of their longitudinal studies of human behavior. They write:

The most dramatic and consistent finding of this study was that many behaviors exhibited by the child during the period 6 to 10 years of age, and a few during the period 3 to 6, were moderately good predictors of theoretically related behaviors during adulthood. Passive withdrawal from stressful situations, dependency on family, ease of anger arousal, involvement in intellectual mastery, social interaction anxiety, sex-role identification, and pattern of sexual behavior in adulthood were each related to reasonably analogous behavioral dispositions during the early years.[4]

On the basis of the above evidence, the need for an organized guidance and counseling program at the elementary level is apparent. Moreover, it appears that there is at least limited recognition and partial support for the idea that the most logical and critical starting point for guidance is in the elementary grades. While the movement has by no means reached ground swell proportions, there has been some notable progress within the past two decades.

[3] Lester N. Downing, *Guidance and Counseling Services: An Introduction* (New York: McGraw-Hill Book Co., 1968), pp. 9–10.

[4] Jerome Kagan, and Howard A. Moss, *Birth to Maturity* (New York: John Wiley & Sons, Inc., 1962), p. 266.

The plan of this book is to deal primarily with the counseling aspects of elementary school guidance; however, in an attempt to place this service in proper perspective it seems advisable to mention briefly the progress of the organized guidance effort in the elementary school. No attempt is made to write a history of elementary school guidance; our purpose in the next section is simply to show that there has been forward movement in the past few years.

Guidance and Counseling in the Elementary School

The growth of organized programs of guidance and counseling in the elementary school is often described as a development of the past two decades. This development epitomizes what Wrenn has called the new look in the elementary school pupil personnel services.[5] The American School Counselor's Association Committee on Elementary School Guidance notes that where guidance at this level was late in starting, its growth during the 1950's and 1960's has been quite rapid.[6]

In 1954, Jones and Miller completed a national study on pupil personnel services in the elementary schools. They reported that 711 full- and part-time counselors were working in the elementary schools at that time.[7] In the same year, Sievers found 254 elementary school counselors working in 354 selected elementary schools.[8] Cottingham, in an article published in 1959, stated that guidance in the elementary school began to develop rapidly during the 1950's.[9] Three years later, Meeks noted that "one of the most important current trends in guidance is the development of organized programs at the elementary level."[10] Again, in 1962, the U.S. Office of Education estimated that 500 counselors were working in the elementary schools of this country.[11] A 1966 report from the U.S. Office of Education revealed that approximately 25 percent of all elementary

---

[5] C. Gilbert Wrenn, *The Counselor in a Changing World* (Washington, D.C.: American Personnel and Guidance Association, 1962), p. 126.

[6] Report of the ASCA Committee on Elementary School Guidance, October, 1964, mimeograph.

[7] Arthur Jones and Leonard Miller, "The National Picture of Pupil Personnel and Guidance Services," *Bulletin No. 38* (Washington, D.C.: National Association of Secondary School Principals, 1954).

[8] Frank Sievers, "Principles and Practices in Elementary School Guidance" (unpublished Ph.D. dissertation, The University of Nebraska, 1954), in Harry Camp, "The Case for Guidance in the Elementary School," *Education,* Vol. 65, No. 7 (March 1955), p. 168.

[9] Harold Cottingham, "Guidance," *The Grade Teacher,* Vol. 79, No. 5 (January 1959), pp. 56–57.

[10] Anna Meeks, "Guidance in The Elementary School," unpublished report, 1963.

[11] Hyrum Smith and Louise O. Eckerson, "Guidance for Children in Elementary Schools," U.S. Office of Education, *Bulletin No. 36* (OE-25032) (Washington, D.C.: U.S. Government Printing Office, 1963).

schools with enrollments over 100 had some services from an elementary "guidance specialist."[12] This report may be somewhat misleading, however, since "guidance specialists" include psychologists and social workers as well as counselors.

A 1967 study of the status of elementary school guidance is appropriate to our discussion here. This survey revealed that approximately 3,800 elementary school counselors are presently working in elementary schools in 48 states. The majority of these counselors are former elementary teachers. Over 70 percent of all counselors in the study were supported in part by federal funds. The study also revealed that 14 states have developed standards for certifying counselors at the elementary level.[13] A more detailed discussion of the status of elementary school guidance is found in Chapter 12.

A most significant development in elementary school counseling is found in the extension of the National Defense Education Act by the 88th Congress. In 1964, Title V of the above act, which provided financial support for secondary school guidance beginning in 1958, was extended to include financial support for guidance and counseling in the elementary school. By the fall of 1965, several states were establishing procedures and criteria for the approval of elementary school guidance programs. A review of the standards established by state departments of education reveals that a strong emphasis is placed upon the counseling function.

Thus it can be seen that organized counseling services for elementary school children are now a reality. Wrenn has characterized these services as an emphasis upon the positive aspects of pupil growth, upon the early identification of pupil characteristics and talents, and upon the developmental needs of all pupils.[14]

The Importance of Counseling in Guidance

The counseling service is widely recognized as a basic component of guidance at the elementary level. Meeks has suggested that the major focus of elementary school guidance should be upon counseling individual pupils and small groups of pupils.[15] Hart found that elementary teachers view counseling individual pupils as a major function

12 Hyrum Smith and Louise O. Eckerson, "Guidance Services in Elementary Schools: A National Survey" U.S. Office of Education, (OE-25045) (Washington, D.C.: U.S. Government Printing Office, 1966).

13 William H. Van Hoose and Catherine M. Vafakas, "A National Survey of Elementary School Guidance," *Personnel and Guidance Journal,* February, 1968, 46:6, pp. 536–539.

14 Wrenn, *op. cit.*

15 Anna R. Meeks, "Guidance in the Elementary School" (Speech delivered at APGA Convention, Denver, Colo., 1960), mimeograph.

of the elementary school guidance worker.[16] McCreary and Miller report that administrators, teachers, and elementary school counselors are in substantial agreement as to the order of importance of the functions of elementary school counselors. All three groups—principals, teachers, and counselors—ranked counseling as the most important function of the elementary counselor.[17]

The 1964 report from the ASCA task force on elementary school guidance places counseling at the top of a list of seven functions of the elementary school counselor. This group emphasizes that all children encounter problems in the process of growing up and that counseling can provide assistance in developing greater self-direction in problem solving. For many children counseling is essential; some find it difficult to meet developmental tasks and others present behavior problems growing out of threats to the child's feelings of security and self-esteem.[18]

The position taken here is that the full-time professional counselor represents the central figure in any good guidance program. It is recognized that many necessary and worthwhile guidance services are performed by the "guidance team"; however, for some children, the complex interaction necessary for personal assistance, self-understanding, and problem solving can occur only in a counseling relationship. Counseling focuses upon the total individual and has as its major aim the longtime adjustment of the counselee. Counseling is a professional task for professionally trained people. While guidance workers carry on many types of activities, counseling contributes to the realization of the objectives of guidance in a more dramatic and personal fashion than the other guidance services. With much justification, counseling is frequently referred to as the "heart" of the guidance program.

Differential Factors in Elementary and Secondary School Counseling

Since the title *elementary school counselor* is a relatively new one, a picture of role differences between the elementary school counselor and his secondary counterpart is just beginning to come into focus. This problem is magnified by the fact that it is only within recent times that professionals in the field have attempted to define the role

[16] Roger N. Hart, "Are Elementary School Counselors Doing the Job?" *The School Counselor,* Vol. 9, No. 2 (December, 1963), pp. 107–10.

[17] William H. McCreary and Gerald Miller, "Elementary School Counselors in California," *Personnel and Guidance Journal,* Vol. 44, No. 5 (January, 1966), pp. 494–99.

[18] Report of the ASCA Committee on Elementary School Guidance, *op. cit.*

of the *secondary* school counselor. Some trends of opinion are emerging, however, and several major differences can now be seen.

Hatch and Costar[19] write that the duties of the elementary school counselor are considerably broader than those of the secondary school counselor. They list four areas of services for the elementary school counselor: (1) to provide guidance services to individual pupils; (2) to consult with school staff; (3) to maintain contacts with the home; and (4) to coordinate the guidance program.

Byrne[20] emphasizes the need for elementary school counselors to have a firm background in psychology as a preparation for their work. He suggests that two years of graduate study is necessary for the professionally competent elementary school counselor. Byrne discusses the elementary counseling function as follows:

> Counselors in the elementary schools serve the basic counseling function of the developmental checkup. In the primary grades their assistance in this is primarily consultative. By the intermediate grades, it is more often a direct experience with pupils. When pupils are identified as deviant, either through the evaluative type of interview or through teacher observation of their behavior, the counselor becomes directly involved.

The 1959 and 1964 *ASCA Reports on Guidance in the Elementary Schools* contains several points which may be used to show some differences between elementary and secondary school counseling. The following points are pertinent to the present discussion:

1. Environmental manipulation is often more necessary when counseling with children. The elementary school counselor must work more closely with the parent and the teacher when planning changes in the environment.
2. The elementary school pupil is less able to assume responsibility for self-study and decision making than the secondary school pupil. This necessitates more direct assistance from the elementary school counselor.
3. The elementary school counselor must have direct understanding of the dynamics of the classroom and of the pupils' activities in the classroom. He must maintain contact with the classroom teacher.
4. A team approach is used to gain understanding of each child so that the instructional program may be geared to take advantage of interests and strengths, and to help motivate the child to overcome weaknesses.

---

[19] Raymond Hatch and James Costar, *Guidance in the Elementary School* (Dubuque, Ia.: Little, Brown and Co., 1961).

[20] R. H. Byrne, *The School Counselor* (Boston: Houghton Mifflin Co., 1963).

Brammer and Shostrom[21] appear to accept most of the above points. They write:

> Children are immature and pliable and when counseling with them it becomes necessary to modify techniques to meet this problem of immaturity. Because the child is immature and not wholly responsible for his actions the counselor must accept some responsibility for directing . . . the client. These factors in no way limit client dignity, value, and unique worthiness as an individual.

Peters has noted that the relative inability of the child to verbalize his feelings and concerns will necessitate some modification of techniques in elementary school counseling. Peters also points out that the dependency factor in the young pupil also accounts for a major difference in elementary and secondary school counseling.[22]

A Point of View

In this book, the term *counseling* will be used to describe the work of a professional counselor whose major function is to assist normal children to maximize their potential for growth. Counseling is viewed as an interpersonal face-to-face relationship between the child and the counselor. Counseling focuses upon the long-time adjustment of the total individual to the kind of environment he will live in.

The counselor is a school staff member, a colleague and consultant to teachers, and a special helper to students. He is not the "school doctor" or the visiting psychologist with a bag of psychodiagnostic puzzles. He is not an itinerant social worker concerned primarily with deviant pupils. The professional school counselor is not the handyman who sweeps up after the principal while keeping one hand in the air to maintain a constant surveillance of the administrative winds. The true professional views himself as a specialist whose primary task is to help students in the school and whose secondary task is to help significant adults do a more effective job in working with children.

The following attitudes are important to his work with children and to his relationships with other professionals in the school.

1. Students are counselees, not patients. Counselees are viewed as normal and healthy, capable of self-understanding and self-direction.

---

21 Lawrence M. Brammer and Everett L. Shostrom, *Therapeutic Psychology,* (Englewood Cliffs, N.J.: Prentice-Hall, Inc., 1960), p. 332.

22 Herman J. Peters, "Differential Factors Between Elementary and Secondary School Counseling," *The School Counselor,* Vol. 7, No. 1 (October, 1959), pp. 3–11.

2. Counseling is viewed as an attempt to produce positive behavior change as well as the development of self-insight.

3. While the counselor, in an attempt to understand his counselees, may need to understand their past, he is basically future oriented. That is, he is more concerned with where the counselee is going than with where he has been.

4. The counselor is concerned with students in all aspects of their development—cognitive, emotional, and vocational. He seeks to help teachers, parents, and others to understand the child as a growing and developing organism.

5. Teachers, administrators, and other professionals are accepted as colleagues equally involved in helping children to become effective members of society. The counselor recognizes and encourages auxiliary services from all school personnel.

It is appropriate in this section to distinguish between counseling normal children in the school and counseling with disturbed children in a mental health or medical setting. In the clinic the counselor (or therapist) generally relies heavily upon such specialized techniques as play therapy, puppetry, and projection. Several factors limit the use of such techniques in the elementary school. Among these limitations are time, physical facilities, and the qualifications of the elementary school counselor. Secondly, since the primary function of the school is instructional, it is questionable whether the clinical type services are justifiable in the elementary school. The elementary school counselor does not seek to produce major changes in personality structure, nor does he anticipate that by virtue of counseling, the counselee will learn to cope with all subsequent problems and difficulties. The emphasis is upon behavior change and the development of self-understanding. Counseling is concerned with helping the counselee maximize learning experiences and with developing and utilizing skills and talents.

The elementary school counselor works with "normal" boys and girls, not with "sick" children. To clarify this point, we assume that most children are normal and healthy. They are able to handle most problems and complexities of life without serious upsets. This does not mean, however, that they can successfully cope with all problems. In fact, most elementary school children, regardless of how normal or how strong, will sometimes find themselves in predicaments that require the services of an adult. The type of service provided during the period when the student is faced with a new and unusual problem can make the difference between healthy development and maladjustment.

It is recognized that some children will have major problems and concerns that may require psychotherapy. However, the elementary school counselor is not a psychotherapist. While he may identify the severely disturbed child, it is unfeasible for him to attempt to apply psychotherapeutic techniques in the elementary school. His function in such cases is to facilitate referral to the appropriate person or agency.

Briefly stated, the position of the author is that the elementary school counselor assists all boys and girls and that this assistance can best be described as developmental. His major concern is the normal pupil and while he does provide limited and indirect services for the seriously maladjusted child, he does not attempt long-term therapy.

Because of the nature of the service he provides, and since he assists large numbers of pupils in the elementary grades, he will use group guidance and group counseling methods as well as individual counseling in achieving the basic goals of guidance at this level.

Selected References

Byrne, R. H. *The School Counselor.* Boston: Houghton Mifflin Co., 1963.

Downing, Lester N. *Guidance and Counseling Services: An Introduction,* New York: McGraw-Hill Book Co., 1968.

Peters, Herman J. "Differential Factors Between Elementary and Secondary School Counseling," *The School Counselor,* Vol. 7, No. 1 (October, 1959), pp. 3–11.

Report of the ASCA Committee on Elementary School Guidance, October, 1964, mimeograph.

Smith, Hyrum, and Eckerson, Louise O. "Guidance Services in Elementary Schools," U.S. Office of Education, *Bulletin No.* OE-25045. Washington, D.C.: U.S. Government Printing Office, 1966.

Van Hoose, William H., and Vafakas, Catherine. "A National Survey of Elementary School Guidance," *Personnel and Guidance Journal* (February, 1968) Vol. 46, p. 6.

PART II

Counseling Content

IF COUNSELING is to be more than a perfunctory task, some understanding of counseling *content* as well as counseling *process* is essential. Content refers to the matter dealt with in counseling and thus gives meaning to the process. Much of the content of counseling with children is derived from such factors as needs, learning, interpersonal relationships, and school learning. Developmental tasks, life stages, and life experiences of the child also provide numerous implications for the content of counseling.

The purpose of Part II is to provide some explanations of behavior which have some relevance for the content of counseling with children. Chapter 2 presents some assumptions about behavior and describes some of the stages and tasks of development. Attention is focused upon cognitive and emotional development. Chapter 3 deals with societal influences upon children and calls attention to those factors which have implications for counseling. The role of the counselor in understanding the child as a member of society and in helping children adapt to changing conditions is emphasized.

The needs of children and youth and the role of the counselor in facilitating learning is discussed in Chapter 4. Since learning is the major concern of the school, this chapter attempts to provide the counselor with some understanding of learning and the learning process.

The material in Part II of this book should help the counselor develop a clearer understanding of counseling content. Further, the following three chapters may suggest some strategies for counselors working with a wide range of socioeconomic and cultural differences.

Chapter 2

Foundations of Behavior: The Individual

IF COUNSELORS are to facilitate smooth and orderly development, they need a clear understanding of the complex processes through which behaviors are developed and modified. Intervention and assistance in changing or modifying behavior necessitates some understanding of its cause. Too, counselors must understand the nature of the learner and the learning process if they are to relate their efforts to total development.

Lacking an understanding of the concept of total development, counselors have too often focused upon the process of counseling without sufficient attention to the substance of the process. Counseling is not an end in itself. The ultimate end is total development of the individual. In fact, the whole purpose of education is to help each individual to achieve a contributive self-actualizing life in a free society. Counseling helps the individual to utilize the process of education to this end.

To recapitulate, meaningful counseling in the elementary school, requires a grasp of the total picture. The counselor will need to be concerned about behavioral processes, the nature of learning, and the conditions that influence learning. Several aspects of behavioral development and the learning process are discussed in this chapter and in Chapters 3 and 4.

Assumptions about Development

Any attempt to explain the nature of the child raises certain philosophical questions which are invariably controversial. There are, however, some very basic ideas about development which any person who works with children and youth must at some time take into consideration. We propose to make a few assumptions here which may help to sensitize the counselor to the complex process of human development.

1. Development is a continuous set of physiological, psychological, and social processes. This development occurs with some regularity and is generally predictable. The child is in a constant state of growing, developing, searching, and becoming.

2. Each phase reflects a range of organizational patterns which occur in a definite sequence within an approximate age span in the continuum of development. The completion of one phase provides some balance for the organism, but as the next phase begins a new imbalance occurs. Performances that build upon developing behaviors are most easily learned.

3. Each individual has the potential capacity for self-fulfillment and the adaptive power to overcome obstacles of his own or of his environment's making. However, each experience within the child's environment has an influence upon his behavior.

4. Effective and healthy development is dependent upon meaningful interaction and communication with others. The child cannot be independent or isolated—he is an interdependent social being. He is not born with the capacity for social interaction. He acquires this capacity through maturation and experience. He must discover and develop his capacity for social warmth and outgoingness.

5. Any interruption or delaying of the normal process of development impairs optimal growth. The fact that one achieves minimally at a given stage may not prepare him to reach the next level.

6. The child is a choice-making being. Beginning very early in life the child is confronted with alternatives and his growth and maturation are intricately involved with the decision-making process. Opportunities for responsible development must also include opportunities for choice making.

7. Adequate adjustment, good mental health, and psychological well-being is related to individual competence and thus is directly related to learning. This concept is discussed in some detail by Grams who asserts that there is a very direct relation-

ship between individual competence and psychological adjustment.[1]

The behavioral processes for counseling purposes encompass both cognitive and affective aspects of development. Behavior is also shaped by the child's interpersonal relationships and by his self-image. All of these mesh into the growing and becoming process.

As stated above, the first requirement for the elementary school counselor is to know something about the developmental growth of his counselees. For our purposes here we have adopted the models of Jean Piaget and Erik H. Erikson who have developed systematic approaches to describing certain developmental processes.

Cognitive Development

Piaget places much emphasis upon cognitive comprehension as a decisive factor in human behavior.[2] His principles of mental growth encompass the stages which children pass through in forming concepts of their experiences. These three stages are summarized below:

1. *The Sensory-Motor Phase* (roughly ages 0–2 years). To Piaget, the sensory-motor phase indicates the infant's creation of a practical world entirely linked to his desires of physical satisfaction. The child can perform only motor actions that form physical schemas which are repeated if they provide a satisfactory experience. This period ends when the child can comprehend that concrete objects can be abstracted into words and thoughts.

2. *The Period of Preparation for Conceptual Thought*
   A. Early (roughly ages 2–4 years). The life of the child during this stage is one of continuous investigation. He investigates his environment and the possibilities for activity within it. Every day he discovers new symbols to use in communication with himself and others. These symbols have primarily a personal reference for him. He does not yet understand the meaning they have in the adult world. Thus, even though the child and the adult may employ the same language they do not necessarily have a common framework for communication.
   B. Later (roughly ages 4–11 years). This is the phase of intuitive thought. During the ages 4–7, children develop

[1] Armin Grams, *Facilitating Learning and Individual Development* (St. Paul, Minn.: Minnesota Department of Education, 1966), p. 18.

[2] For material for this section, the author has relied heavily upon the work of John H. Flavell, *The Developmental Psychology of Jean Piaget* (Princeton, N.J.: D. Van Nostrand Co., Inc., 1963), and Henry W. Maier, *Three Theories of Child Development* (New York: Harper & Row, Publishers, 1965).

an increasing interest in the world around them. Repeated contacts with other children and with adults reduces egocentricity and increases social participation. By the time the child enters school, his thinking is largely the verbalization of his mental processes. Just as he once used his motor apparatus to act out his thinking, he now employs speech to express himself. His perception and interpretation of his environment are continuously colored by his personal preconceptions and may be at variance with reality and with adults. Generally he can deal with only one idea at a time.

Roughly during the ages 7–11, the child achieves a new level of mental function; namely *operational thought*. Operational thought refers to the ability to relate experience to an organized whole. Mental experimentation, however, still depends upon perception. The child in the 7–11-year-age range generally cannot perform mental operations unless he can perceive their inner logicality. The child in this stage is able to abstract the meaning of words to letter symbols, and he begins to shift from an inductive to a deductive mode of thinking.[3]

3. *The Phase of Cognitive Thought* (roughly age 11 and up). The final phase of intellectual development occurs sometime between the ages of 11–15 years, marking the end of childhood and the beginning of the youth phase. During this stage the individual begins to think and reason beyond his own realistic world. He enters the world of ideas and acquires the capacity to think. Cognition begins to rely upon pure symbolism and the use of propositions rather than sole reality. Cognitive random behavior is replaced by a systematic approach to problem solving. The youth develops the capacity to reason by hypothesis and thus has a new tool to understand his physical world and his social relationships within it.[4]

In Piagetan concepts, intellectual development is irrevocably tied up with personality development. He suggests that the faculty of knowing serves as the coordinator, and occupies a position parallel to the synthetic function of the ego in an analytic formation. All attributes of personality depend upon the mental capacity of the individual to organize his experiences.[5]

---

[3] Maier, op. cit., pp. 115–16.

[4] *Ibid.*, pp. 135–37.

[5] Jean Piaget, *Origins of Intelligence in Children* (New York: W. W. Norton & Co., Inc., 1963).

Implications for Counseling

How can the elementary school counselor put Piaget's conceptual stages to use in working with children? Gowan, Coole, and McDonald believe that counselors who become familiar with Piaget's work on child development will possess new means for understanding children. While many counselors have been using the idea of cognitive competence for a long time, the lack of a model has prevented them from knowing whether what they were doing was right. The intuitive counselor is like the man who could find the cat in the dark room, and Piaget is like the man who turned on the light so that we can all see where the cat is. The above authors further stress the importance of cognitive competence to mental health. They write:

> 1. At certain stages in the child's development, it is cognitive competence, rather than emotional development which is central.
>
> 2. Cognitive competence is the child's chief mainstay to reality, and hence the chief bulwark of his general emotional stability. Conversely, cognitive competence is the chief precursor of emotional stability.
>
> 3. Cognitive development on schedule is conducive to emotional health and a proper self-concept, and a lack of cognitive development on schedule is conducive to emotional disturbance and lack of a proper self-concept.
>
> 4. Cognitive development may be stimulated by proper and appropriate curriculum experiences directed toward the student's particular abilities and stage of concept development.
>
> 5. Cognitive competence can be enhanced by proper and appropriate guidance experiences that emphasize the development of realistic and optimistic self-concepts.
>
> 6. Guidance efforts to promote cognitive competence involve *(a)* sympathetic and supportive individual attention, *(b)* promotion by the counselor of a student's ability to make changes in his self-concepts through changes in his relationships, and *(c)* remedial retraining in basic skills.[6]

While Piaget's theory furnishes the counselor with a frame of reference for understanding the counselee, a word of caution is in order. First, the theory in itself is inadequate for understanding children and must be supplemented by other concepts. Secondly, at

---

[6] John C. Gowan, Doris Coole, and Peggy McDonald, "The Impact of Piaget on Guidance," *Elementary School Guidance and Counseling,* Vol. 1, No. 3 (June, 1967), pp. 212–13.

the appraisal level the counselor may wish to evaluate his counselees on the basis of personal competence rather than on the basis of the more restricted concept, cognitive competence. In fact, emotional competence may be equally important to adequate development.

Other authors have raised questions regarding the appropriateness of Piaget's developmental stages. For example, Cronbach feels that the location of the stages on a continuum represents an oversimplification. He points out that there are no sharp transition points between stages of development. Further, when trying to learn something new the individual must gradually work his way from one step to the next. He does not move abruptly from intuitive to operational thought and he cannot deal in abstractions without a base of experience.[7]

Basically, the developmental trends of Piaget and others describe individual potentiality. The actual developmental profile of any child will show peaks in some areas and depressions in others. In addition, numerous variations will exist between students of the same age and in the same class.

Emotional Development

The emotions play a major role in the life of the child. They color his everyday experiences, they influence his perceptions of his environment and the people in it, and serve as a motivation to action. The emotional reactions which a child experiences develop into habit patterns and as such become driving forces in behavior.

Childhood is a critical stage in the development of emotions. Children who have pleasant and satisfying experiences are, for the most part, better adjusted adolescents and adults.

The intensive work of Erik H. Erikson on emotional development can be extremely valuable to elementary school counselors in their attempts to understand more of child development. Erikson believes that the emotional aspects of life permeate all human functions. The nature of emotional content and the quality of interpersonal relationships, determines the basic core of man's makeup. He stresses that the same factors which make for healthy interpersonal relationships also contribute to pathological relationships. Personality disturbance is an imbalance in the total emotional makeup of the individual.

Erikson emphasizes the impact of the family and society upon emotional development. The child-rearing practices of a society serve

[7] Lee J. Cronbach, *Educational Psychology* (New York: Harcourt, Brace & World, Inc., 1963), p. 338.

to preserve the group's unique qualities and at the same time strives to keep the dependent child alive. "The growing child must, at every step, derive a vitalizing sense of actuality from the awareness that his individual way of mastering experience is a successful variant of a group identity and is in accord with its space-time and life plan."[8]

To Erikson development is an evolutional process based upon a universally experienced sequence of biological, psychological, and social events. In general, Erikson's developmental stages coincide with standard ranges of chronological and sociocultural age groupings. In each stage of development, the individual must face and master a central task which becomes dominant, and which reveals itself in the clearest form as his dilemma during that stage. When this developmental task or problem is solved, the individual can move on to the next stage. Thus, development is a continuous process, with each phase equally a part of the continuum. Each stage is related to the previous phase and each plays a vital role in the total scheme of development. In Erikson's view they are also stages of constant motion. The individual never *has* a personality; he is constantly developing and redeveloping his personality. His stages of psychosocial development are summarized below.

Erikson:

1. *The Sense of Trust.* The first important quality the individual develops is a sense of trust, which usually emerges during the first year of life. During this stage the child comes to feel that he can rely upon much of the world to be predictable and consistent. Fortunately most infants have little trouble developing this all-important sense of trust because their needs at this stage are nearly always satisfied.

2. *The Sense of Autonomy.* When the child is about 12 or 15 months old he begins trying to assert his individuality. This struggle is particularly intense during the next two years. He should feel that he is an adequate human being, self-reliant, but nevertheless able to use the help and guidance of others in many important matters. During this stage adults need to be consistent both in what they permit and forbid him to do.

3. *The Sense of Initiative.* Having established himself as an individual in his own right, the four- to five-year-old must seek to discover how much he can do. Because his conscience has started to develop, his behavior is guided at least partly by his notions of right and wrong. At no other time in life does the individual learn so willingly. These first three stages are probably the most important in life.

---

[8] Erik H. Erikson, *Childhood and Society* (2d ed.; New York: W. W. Norton & Co., Inc., 1963), p. 235.

4. *The Sense of Duty and Accomplishment.* During the years from 6 to 12, the child tends increasingly to engage in tasks that are socially useful. This stage is a time of calm, steady growth. The chief danger at this point is that he may develop a sense of inferiority if too much or too little is expected of him.

5. *The Sense of Identity.* The problem of identity is central during adolescence, when rapid physiological changes contribute to inner turmoil. Faced with confusion in his status the adolescent often seeks security by fostering similarity to others in his age group.

6. *The Sense of Intimacy.* Only a person who is sure of his own identity can share satisfying relationships with others—in either the form of friendship or love. American culture stresses individuality, duty, and identity much more than the sense of intimacy.

7. *The Parental Sense.* Characterized by an interest in one's offspring.

8. *The Sense of Integrity.* The sense of one's role in life.[9]

Erikson attaches major importance to the early stages of development. He believes that if all goes well during these critical periods, the individual will have a foundation which will help to sustain him throughout life.

The third stage encompasses only two years of the child's life (ages 4–5) and corresponds roughly to the nursery school and kindergarten years. Erikson describes this stage as a time when the child seems to "grow together" both in his person and in his body. He is more himself, more loving, relaxed, and brighter in judgment, more activated, and more activating. He can forget failure and frustration and approach that which seems desirable with more purpose and more certainty.[10] It is a time of initiative and of testing limits. It is also a critical time of sex-role identification. According to Erikson, the one major danger in this period, for boys, is the inevitable failure in rivalry with the father, which if too crushing, will lead to a pervasive sense of guilt.

The fourth stage of development is most important to our discussion here in that it encompasses the elementary school years, ages 6–12. As Erikson puts it, the child is "now set for the 'entrance into life,' except that life must first be school life, whether school is field, or jungle, or classroom."[11] He is now ready to adapt himself to specific tasks and skills and can become an eager and absorbed unit of a productive situation. He begins to develop a sense of *industry*.

9 *Ibid.,* pp. 247–69.
10 *Ibid.,* p. 255.
11 *Ibid.,* p. 258.

The danger in this period lies in a sense of inadequacy to develop the skills required. If he becomes discouraged or develops feelings of inferiority regarding his skills or his status among peers he may withdraw to the more isolated world of the previous stage.

In a discussion of Erikson's theory, Maier writes that the developmental stages constitute the ego's timetable and mirror the structure of the relevant social institutions. To paraphase Maier:

An individual develops into the next phase as soon as he is biologically, psychologically, and socially ready, and his individual readiness is matched by societal readiness. Each phase introduces a new set of the intensive encumbrances of society and, together, these phases embrace a series of encumbrances that are instituted in human life. There are three essential variables. First, the inner laws of development which, like biological processes, are irreversible; second, the cultural influences which specify the desirable rate of development and favor certain aspects of the inner laws at the expense of others; and third, the idiosyncratic response of each individual and his particular way of handling his development in response to society's demands. It should be pointed out that temporary regression in any of the several major areas of development is considered to be a natural by-product of the developmental process. To cite Erikson's faith in the power of the ego, we quote this optimistic comment: "Children 'fall apart' repeatedly, and unlike Humpty Dumpty, grow together again."[12]

Heffernan, in an adaptation of Erikson's concepts, has likened the eight stages to tasks which the individual must achieve in order to develop a healthy personality.[13] The eight major attainments are not, of course, confined to the age periods mentioned. Once achieved, each attainment continues to develop throughout life. The apex of development is the last stage, the stage of integrity.

Implications for Counseling

Helping children, on either a formal counseling level, or on the guidance level, includes working with the individual's past, his present level of development, and the quality of his ongoing relationships. Further, the counselor must give due consideration to factors outside the school and their influence upon the child's development. The following propositions characterize some understandings necessary to effective work with children.

---

12 Maier, *op. cit.*, p. 29.

13 Helen Heffernan, "The Organization of the Elementary School and the Development of a Healthy Personality," *Calif. J. of Elem. Ed.*, Vol. 20 (1952), pp. 129–153.

1. The quality of the child's interpersonal relationships need to be ascertained and evaluated.
2. The family and various sociocultural factors are major influences upon behavior. An understanding of these forces is vital to effective counseling.
3. The behavior of any child at any given time is intricately tied up to his feelings about himself, his environment, and the key people in his life. Consequently, help from the counselor may be ineffective unless these perceptions are dealt with.
4. Counseling may require an assessment of the child's developmental status with a particular focus upon the stages which are of major significance at the time. The key for intervention is to be found in the child's developmental status.
5. It is often necessary to help the child indirectly by affecting certain key environmental influences in his life. This includes working with parents, teachers, and others involved in the life of the child. The focus is not upon psychological help for the adult, however; the counselor's effort is directed toward helping the adult adjust and enrich his relationships with the child.

The Self-Concept

As the child grows, develops, experiences, and interacts with significant others, he develops a concept of himself, or a self-image. As Frank has stated: "The child learns to think and feel about himself as defined by others. He develops an image of himself as the chief actor in a private world. This image develops primarily from the way parents, teachers, and significant others describe, punish, praise, or love him."[14] For full acceptance, the child learns that he must develop personal competence and that he must become productive. He discovers that success in school, sharing, fair play, and the ability to solve problems win recognition and approval.

In school, his work is constantly evaluated, praised, and criticized. He learns that some performances win praise and others do not. He acquires standards by which to judge himself and an ideal of what society expects a good person to be. If his performances and conduct are accepted, he comes to believe that he is a good person. If he senses failure and seems never to approach the ideal, he develops a feeling of inadequacy. A healthy self-concept is, to quote Cronbach, "I am adequate to meet present demands upon me, and where I want to do better, I can do better."[15]

---

[14] L. K. Frank, *Your Adolescent at Home and School* (New York: The Viking Press, Inc., 1956) in Elizabeth B. Hurlock, *Child Development,* p. 526.

[15] Cronbach, *op. cit.,* p. 126.

In working with children and youth, it is necessary to keep in mind that the individual's concept of himself is a prime determinant of behavior. Either a poor self-concept, or an overconfident, unrealistic self-concept leads to poor adjustment. The negative influence of seeing oneself as inadequate and inferior is well documented. Several authorities have consistently emphasized that unfavorable self-acceptance leads to poor school achievement, low aspiration, a negative attitude toward school, and frustration and doubts about one's future.

While the school curriculum probably provides the primary vehicle for the development of adequate self-concepts and the alteration of negative self-images, guidance and counseling services are also necessary. This is particularly so at the elementary level when children are still at the formative stage. Working directly with youngsters on a counseling basis, with the objective of helping them explore the meaning and appropriateness of feelings about self, can be a potent force in reconstructing negative self-attitudes. The developmental counselor will also extend his services to parents and teachers in an effort to help them understand their role in helping children develop appropriate self-images.

Maladjustive Behaviors

While the school counselor is concerned primarily with "normal" healthy children, at times he will find it necessary to work with "maladjusted" youngsters. Further, his role as a consultant will also demand indirect services for problem youngsters through work with adults who are involved in the child's life.

The author recognizes some of the pitfalls in using the overworked term "maladjusted." As Ginsburg has pointed out, too often the term implies that a person is sick and a drain on society. Also, when discussing children, it is often assumed that absence of "good" adjustment is a sure sign of trouble. Ginsburg states: "Adjustment must always be thought of in relative terms: in terms of who and when and where and under what circumstances."[16]

For our purposes here, it should be emphasized that we are not speaking of the "sick" child who needs psychiatric help; neither are we dealing with the behavior which occasionally deviates from a presumed norm. Obviously the school counselor is not equipped to deal with the sick child. But the normal child is not well adjusted all the time.

---

[16] Sol W. Ginsburg, *A Psychiatrist's Views on Social Issues* (New York: Columbia University Press, 1963), p. 48.

Normal includes a wide range of behaviors, and to the extent that some of these behaviors differ significantly from the norm, they become troublesome, unusual, or abnormal. Generally they are transitory in nature and can be treated through counseling in the school. Broadly speaking, there are two conditions which create problems for children who fit in the category described above. Each condition requires some assistance from adults.

The first condition results when the home or school fails to provide opportunities for the child to develop a sense of trust, a sense of personal identity, a feeling of competence and accomplishment, and an appropriate self-image. Such children are vulnerable to the development of maladjustive behavior. Children who are rejected, severely punished, ridiculed, and deprived of meaningful human relationships, tend to react with negativism, withdrawal, overaggressiveness, irresponsibility, and generally destructive rather than constructive behavior. Failure in school and rejection in the peer group also contribute to negative behavior and poor adjustment.

The second condition involves the child overwhelmed by experiences and events in his everyday life which he is unable to manage successfully. Most children at some time during the elementary grades find themselves in situations which are unusual. They may not be prepared to handle these unusual problems. Consider for example, the trauma of divorce or the death of a loved one. Consider also what happens when a child meets his first disappointment or first failure. Although many children may handle such stress without noticeable difficulty, others may well fall apart temporarily.[17] Redl makes this point in the following comment:

> . . . destiny does not use clinical judgment about how much [stress] a given child can manage on his own at a given time. Just as in our own lives, in theirs too, things sometimes pile up. The point is, if the pile up comes to a certain child at a certain age, it is important that an adult be nearby to help the child cope with these overwhelming experiences.
>
> Regardless of how healthy or normal the youngster, during the onslaught of certain experiences; . . . normal youngsters are more similar to the legitimately disturbed ones than to their own normal selves.[18]

Summary

In the foregoing discussion, the author has relied heavily upon the theories of Piaget and Erikson for an explanation of child behavior.

---

[17] Fritz Redl discusses this concept at some length in *When We Deal with Children* (New York The Free Press, 1966), pp. 63–64.

[18] *Ibid.,* p. 64.

While the two theories of child development are based upon a different cluster of assumptions, they are in many respects mutually compatible. It is felt that the two theories supplement each other and that together they provide the elementary school counselor with a solid base for understanding total development.

Both Piaget and Erikson believe in the regularity of human growth and development. They emphasize that human life unfolds in an orderly process and in predictable ways. Each theorist grants the individual the potential capacity to make his own decisions and to solve his own problems. Both Piaget and Erikson speak of the unfolding of the developmental processes during which all new development finds its roots in previous acquisitions.

An understanding of cognitive development is vital to elementary school counselors. However, an understanding of intellectual functions alone would prove inadequate. Knowledge of emotional and interpersonal processes will supplement this understanding and aid in our efforts to assist children through counseling.

The emphasis in this chapter has been upon normal healthy development. However, it is recognized that some children, because of inadequate opportunities and outside experiences, do not develop normally. In such cases, the elementary school counselor intervenes in an attempt to prevent or modify deviant development.

Selected References

CRONBACH, LEE J. *Educational Psychology.* New York: Harcourt, Brace & World, Inc., 1963.

ERIKSON, ERIK H. *Childhood and Society.* 2d ed.; New York: W. W. Norton & Co., Inc., 1963.

FLAVELL, JOHN H. *The Developmental Psychology of Jean Piaget.* Princeton, N.J.: D. Van Nostrand Co., Inc., 1963.

GOWAN, JOHN C., COOLE, DORIS, and MCDONALD, PEGGY. "The Impact of Piaget on Guidance," *Elementary School Guidance and Counseling,* Vol. 1, No. 3 (June, 1967), pp. 212–13.

MAIER, HENRY W. *Three Theories of Child Development.* New York: Harper & Row, Publishers, 1965.

PIAGET, JEAN. *Origins of Intelligence in Children.* New York: W. W. Norton & Co., Inc., 1963.

Chapter 3

Foundations of Behavior: Society

ONE OF THE MAJOR ARGUMENTS favoring guidance and counseling in schools is that children and youth need assistance in understanding themselves, and the world in which they will live. The transition from childhood to adolescence and finally to adult status poses complex and sometimes ambiguous problems. In a society characterized by rapid changes and shifting standards, the need to help youth learn to cope with both their present and future world takes on added significance.

Throughout this book it is emphasized that children are adaptable and that they can be helped to develop along positive lines. In short, with proper assistance during the formative stages of development, the adult of tomorrow can exercise a large measure of control over his own destiny. The elementary school counselor can be the critical additive in helping today's children become the competent adults of tomorrow.

The problems confronting children and youth in becoming adults is not a uniquely American phenomenon. To paraphrase Erikson, most cultures make fairly definite demands upon the individual. At each age level there are certain requirements which the individual must meet in order to adapt to his society. In the final analysis, the growing individual unites biological, psychological, and social forces. Man is, thus, at all times an organism, an ego, and a member of society and is simultaneously involved in all three processes of organization.[1]

The major purpose of this chapter is to discuss the impact of various social phenomena upon the development and education of children. More specifically, attention will be focused upon those elements which influence the counseling and guidance needs of elementary school children. The following elements require special consideration:

1. Social complexity and change.
2. The family and its influences.
3. Social class influences.
4. Changes in education.
5. The world of work.
6. Inner city and outer city.
7. Implications for counseling.

Social Complexity and Change

Before considering the above points in detail it may be helpful to mention some of the major factors which influence all social change in this country. To cite Wrenn: "Some of these (factors) are contrasting. We believe in material progress, in new things, but we also devoutly believe in *people*, their rights, their freedom of choice, their education."[2]

Wrenn describes three relatively new and powerful influences upon social change: (1) the scientific mode of thought, (2) the search for a sense of direction, and (3) a sense of nearness to the rest of the world. Wrenn believes that the most pervasive of these influences is the scientific mode of thought. Science is much more than technology. The scientist, in search of the truth, finds that scientific truth is not absolute; that what we know today may be obsolete tomorrow. These developments lead to the sacrifice of some of our most cherished beliefs, and create uncertainties for the individual.[3]

Wrenn comments upon our search for meaning as follows:

---

[1] Erik Erikson, *Childhood and Society* (2d ed.; New York: W. W. Norton & Co., Inc., 1963), p. 36.

[2] C. Gilbert Wrenn, *The Counselor in a Changing World* (Washington, D.C.: American Personnel and Guidance Association, 1962), p. 12.

[3] *Ibid.*, p. 12.

The search for purpose is both national and personal—perhaps the one within the other. It is as though a family had gone through its physical growing stages, had a home and income, had children who were now half-grown and who were asking, "What's it all about, Pa?" We are uneasily aware that we have grown very fast, have our feet on solid economic and democratic ground, but can't see the next steps clearly.[4]

Scientific achievements, such as rapid transoceanic transportation and communications satellites, have rendered the traditional geographic isolation of America an impossibility. Living and interacting with people from over 100 other countries is now a fact of life. We can no longer feel secure in our belief that we are omnipotent and immune to problems that beset other nations. These conditions raise the question of whether we can control our own destiny. This condition can be an unsettling experience and can make us aware of the need to consider carefully several aspects of our own society. It is impossible, of course, to know exactly what will take place in the future, but on the basis of present conditions and trends some predictions can be made with a reasonable degree of accuracy.

In the first place it is clear that there will be many more people in the next two decades. We have been in the midst of a population explosion for some time and at the present rate of increase the population of the United States is expected to reach 250 million by 1980. If present trends continue, the great masses that make up our present cities will have forced the cities to expand until they meet. This doesn't mean that everyone will live in the city, but it does suggest that few people will live far from a city. Rural America is rapidly disappearing, and with it will go a way of life.[5]

Technological changes will have a major impact upon the world of work and upon people's lives. Michael comments upon one important area, the life sciences. During the next two decades more people will be working in life sciences, in such fields as genetics, brain processes, growth and aging; they will almost certainly make discoveries as dramatic as the ones the physical scientists—the atom smashers and the space experts—have made so far in this century.

In medicine, for example, we can expect further conquest of disease, advances in surgical techniques, and development of new drugs more powerful than the antibiotics and personality changers introduced during the last 20 years. Late in the period, biologists probably will discover how to change inherited characteristics; they may also make it possible to predetermine a baby's sex or, at least, to

---

[4] *Ibid.*, p. 12.

[5] Donald M. Michael, *Your Child and the World of Tomorrow* (Washington, D.C.: National Education Association, 1966).

increase the possibilities that the baby will be of the sex its parents prefer.

Automation will become increasingly important in our lives. Not only does automation make it possible to produce more, automation also makes it possible to produce items that would be too expensive if the work had to be done by man. Automation also makes it possible to produce items which human hands simply cannot handle—infinitesimal electronic parts, for example.

Just as automated processes can outproduce man's hands and senses, so computers can, in some ways, outproduce his brain. Computers make it possible to put to use the enormous amounts of information that come from the laboratories of our complex society. The use of automation and computers will enable us to do more work in less time. As a result, many more people will have more leisure time.[6]

While the school counselor cannot reverse present trends, he can help children and youth learn to live with some of the uncertainties resulting from rapid social change. Stewart and Warnath write that the counselor can help the student understand what the future holds and make plans relative to it.[7]

2 The Family and Its Influences

The American family structure has undergone vast changes within the past few decades. These changes are the result of urbanization, improvement in the economy, changes in the traditional method of work at home, changes in the husband-wife relationship, both in terms of increased equality for women and the decrease in male authority, and a breakdown in family consciousness. Ginsburg[8] summarizes Burgess who has noted the following changes in the American family:

human equality

A downgrading of the authority of parents; a trend toward egalitarianism in relations between the male and the female, with a relative decrease in the authority of the father; parental uncertainty; decline in the importance of relatives; and the irresponsibility of children.

More recently, Bronfenbrenner has noted the following changes in the American family:

---

6 *Ibid.*

7 Lawrence H. Stewart and Charles F. Warnath, *The Counselor and Society* (Boston: Houghton Mifflin Co., 1965), pp. 87–88.

8 Sol W. Ginsburg, *A Psychiatrist's Views on Social Issues* (New York: Columbia University Press, 1963), p. 195.

1. Families are smaller.
2. Relationships with relatives are weaker.
3. More mothers work outside the home.
4. The father is often absent from the home.
5. Social mobility and vocational mobility have increased.
6. Recreation has moved out of the home.
7. Responsibilities for child rearing have shifted to outside agencies.
8. Child-rearing practices are more democratic.

Bronfenbrenner, commenting upon child-rearing responsibilities of parents writes:

Children *used* to be brought up by their parents . . . But *de facto* responsibility for upbringing has shifted from the family to other settings in society. While the family still has the primary moral and legal responsibility for developing character in children, the power or opportunity to do the job is often lacking in the home, primarily because parents and children no longer spend enough time together in those situations in which such training is possible. This is not because parents don't want to spend time with their children. It is simply that conditions of life have changed.[9]

Psychologists, anthropologists, and educators all recognize the importance of family life and family experiences upon the development of the child's behavior and attitudes. Because the home is the child's first environment, and since the first social learning begins in the home, it sets the pattern for the child's attitudes toward people, things, and the world in general. Further, the child identifies with certain family members, imitates their behavior and adjusts to life as they adjust. Inconsistencies, problems, and anxieties within the home will thus have negative influences upon the child. Some areas of the child's life on which the family and family conditions have major influences are as follows:

1. THE SELF-CONCEPT. Unfavorable home conditions and poor family relationships often lead to negative self-concepts and poor adjustment. Children are quick to sense an unhealthy or neurotic psychological climate in the home and such conditions affect the child emotionally, intellectually, and physically. Children from broken homes or homes where parents are "emotionally divorced" develop attitudes and behavior patterns that interfere with adjustment to school.

By contrast, wholesome family relationships lead to positive self-concept, and good personal and school adjustment. As Tyler *et al.*

---

[9] Urie Bronfenbrenner, "The Split Level American Family," *Saturday Review*, October 7, 1967, p. 60.

has pointed out, motivation and personal adjustment are directly related to preschool experiences.[10]

2. SCHOOL SUCCESS. The child's performance in school and his attitude toward school is directly affected by his experiences in the family. Rejection and overpunitiveness on the part of family members leads to insecurity and poor school work. Family disturbances have a particularly serious effect upon school work which requires thinking. A lack of interest in the child's education or a low regard for education on the part of parents or other significant family members has a retarding effect upon the child's progress in school.

3. SOCIAL ADJUSTMENT. The first social learning takes place in the home and is directly affected by family attitudes and relationships. During the first years of life, the child begins to learn the meaning of cooperation, group living, and group behavior. The child who experiences poor affectional relationships in the home may develop cold, suspicious attitudes, and will thus have difficulty establishing meaningful relationships outside the home. Strict and overpunitive parents contribute to hostile and aggressive behavior in children. Likewise, overprotectiveness on the part of parents can lead to dependent and docile children. Homes where the atmosphere is democratic and where there are happy relationships between family members foster the development of behavior conducive to good social relationships.

The point of this discussion is that social learning and social development is crucial to school learning and to total development. Again, it should be emphasized that the school also has a responsibility for social learning. Further the school can intervene directly in cases where children need help in overcoming previous inadequacies in social learning and adjustment. The school can also intervene indirectly through helping parents change their relationships with the child.

4. VOCATIONAL ASPIRATIONS. One of the critical problems facing education is to help students pursue educational and vocational goals commensurate with their capacity and talent. As Roe has pointed out, many of the child's attitudes toward different types of vocations are a direct result of parental influence. Thus, the vocational success of the individual will be determined largely by the attitudes toward work established in the home when he was a child.[11]

---

10 F. B. Tyler, J. E. Lafferty, and B. B. Tyler, "Relationships among Motivations of Parents and Their Children," *Journal of Genetic Psychology,* Vol. 101 (1962), pp. 69–81.

11 Ann Roe, "Early Determinants of Vocational Choice," *Journal of Counseling Psychology* Vol. 4 (1957), pp. 212–17.

This problem takes on added significance in the case of children in the lower socioeconomic groups. The psychological effects of living with parents with low-status jobs or who are unemployed, are generally those of a poor self-image and low-level vocational aspiration. Quite often a special approach to changing both vocational aspiration and vocational self-concept is necessary.

Social Class Influences

It is now an established fact that the behavior of children and youth is greatly influenced by the cultural setting in which they grow and develop. This point is well documented in anthropological studies of Kluckhohn[12] which show that behavior should be judged in relation to the cultural setting in which it occurs.

Any person who has worked with young people from a variety of backgrounds will be aware of the socioeconomic variations in behavior. Some behaviors, while accepted and expected in one social class setting, may be viewed as reprehensible in another. For example, some teachers may not understand or accept certain behaviors of children from lower status subcultures. It should also be emphasized that differences also contribute to wide variations in achievement motivation, in attitudes toward school, and of even greater import, in the youngster's concept of self.

Landes has written that effective work with students from different cultural backgrounds is most difficult unless these cultural differences are clearly understood. For example, she feels that attempting to counsel in a nondirective, nonauthoritarian manner with a child accustomed to adults who are very direct and authoritarian, may lead the child to believe that the adult is weak and incompetent.[13] This illustration raises some questions that cannot be completely answered. It should be obvious, however, that the counselor should be aware of cultural influences upon his counselees and the implications of these differences for counseling and guidance. There are some cautions, however, which the counselor should understand.

One of the potential dangers in ascribing behavior to cultural forces is the tendency to blame behavior on the culture and then assume that nothing can be done to change it. Such reasoning is, of course, false. In the first place, there are other factors, (i.e., biological and intellectual) that influence behavior. Secondly, strategic interferences can help the child learn the positive behaviors that lead to the development of more desirable characteristics.

---

[12] Clyde Kluckhohn, *Mirror for Man* (New York: McGraw-Hill Book Co., 1949).

[13] Ruth Landes, "An Anthropologist Looks at School Counseling," *Journal of Counseling Psychology,* Vol. 10 (1963), pp. 14–17.

A second danger which overlaps the first, is the tendency to label certain values and standards as "upper class," "middle class," "lower class," etc., as though one class has exclusive claim to certain dispositions and actions. This is a gross oversimplification. In fact, it may be that the stereotype "class" is no longer valid. For example, there is some question as to whether an "upper class" exists in our society. Further it seems probable that the various differences between the several socioeconomic groups in our country will diminish with an increase in access to the same opportunities. It is not socioeconomic class per se which influences behavior; rather it is learning or the lack of learning which determines the relationship between socioeconomic class and behavior. Granted that learning, or more accurately socialization, begins in the home, and the family environment is a vital influencer of behavior. Different approaches and emphases in the socialization process can be ascribed, in some measure at least, to socioeconomic class. However, it is the child-rearing practice employed in the subculture and not socioeconomic class which provides the discriminating variable for child behavior. Child-rearing practices and their relevance for counseling are discussed in some detail in Chapter 9.

Changes in Education

Several years ago the President's Commission on Education described the purposes of education as follows:

> Education is an institution of every civilized society, but the purposes of education are not the same in all societies. An educational system finds its guiding principles and ultimate goals in the aims and philosophy of the social order in which it functions. The two predominant types of society in the world today are the democratic and the authoritarian, and the social role of education is very different in the two systems.
>
> American society is a democracy: that is, its folkways and institutions, its arts, sciences and religions are based on the principle of equal freedom for all its members, regardless of race, faith, sex, economic, or occupational status. The law of the land, providing equal justice for the poor as well as the rich, for the weak as well as the strong is one instrument by which a democratic society establishes, maintains, and protects equality among different persons and groups. The other instrument is education, which as all leaders in the making of democracy have pointed out again and again, is necessary to give effect to the equality prescribed by law.[14]

---

[14] The President's Commission on Education, *Higher Education for American Democracy* (Washington, D.C.: U.S. Government Printing Office, 1947), Vol. 1, p. 5.

The above statement was issued two decades ago. The principles enunciated above still hold true today, however. The challenge is not in the acceptance of the fundamental principles of education; the real challenge to education and to society is in developing educational plans and programs for implementing the principle of "education for all." In spite of several misinformed and verbose critics, there is much evidence that the educational institution in this country has produced a product far superior to that produced by schools in most other countries. At the same time, American public schools have attempted to provide meaningful education for *all* children. This is consistent with our democratic ideals. To paraphrase Mortensen and Schmuller, one attempt to assist all students to develop to the fullest of their capacities in terms of the democratic ideal is through the provision of specialized guidance services.[15]

The American public school has changed drastically over the past two decades. While this change may be more evolutionary than revolutionary, there is no doubt that schools are deeply involved in the broader social revolution. Some of the more visible changes of major concern to the counselor are discussed below.

1. CHANGES IN THE CURRICULUM. There are numerous signs of change in today's elementary school curriculum. Curriculum innovators are offering instructional kits, programmed materials, televised lessons, and other aids as an alternative to the traditional textbook. Pronounced changes are also apparent in mathematics and foreign language programs for children. The new materials offer a new form, but frequently fail to provide new content. Wrenn points out that the introduction of new curriculum content is necessary to meet changing conditions in our culture as well as meeting changes within an area of knowledge. He suggests that the counselor should be knowledgeable about changes in the student population and about the specific community cultures from which students come. The counselor can then share this information and point out implications for curricular development.[16]

2. CHANGING EMPHASIS ON THE ROLE OF THE SCHOOL. The school is no longer concerned only with intellectual development of the pupil. The school now recognizes its obligation for developing intellectual, social, and vocational competence. The development of competencies in all three areas is necessary to the development of *personal* competency which is the major goal of education in the first place.

---

[15] Donald G. Mortensen and Allen N. Schmuller, *Guidance in Today's Schools* (New York: John Wiley & Sons, Inc., 1959), p. 3.

[16] Wrenn, *op. cit.*, p. 93.

The elementary school counselor has a vital role to play in helping children develop these three competencies. The school and the counselor must be concerned with intellectual growth both from the standpoint of the needs of the individual and the needs and demands of society. At the same time the counselor must respond to the student's need to develop social and vocational competency but neither to the exclusion of the other.

3. CHANGES IN STAFF AND SERVICES. Teachers and administrators are no longer the only professional workers in the schools. A third professional group—the pupil personnel workers—are now accepted as integral members of the school staff. Counselors, psychologists, remedial specialists, social workers, speech therapists and others are now complementing the work of teachers. These professionals have been added in response to a growing need for more personalized and individualized assistance for students. Society's demands, today and tomorrow, will undoubtedly create a need for more professionals who can provide services essential for aiding children and youth to acquire the personal competencies mentioned above. Thus, the child will have vital assistance from a number of professionals.

While changes in education are necessary to meet the demands of a changing society, we must not forget that we are educating children, not producing robots. Arbuckle has cautioned that educating children is not the same as the assembly-line production of an automobile. Children can learn only so much in any given time when children are accepted as children, rather than treated as miniature adults.[17] It may be that some schools have already placed too much emphasis upon academic growth. Obviously some balance is needed and the school counselor may be one professional who can help provide that balance.

THE WORLD OF WORK

Children presently in the elementary grades will sooner or later enter the adult world of work. Preparation for the world of work is a long and complex process that begins early in life. Assisting young people to acquire the understanding and to develop the attitudes necessary for selecting a job suitable to one's abilities and talents is a major responsibility of the school. This task becomes more difficult in light of major changes in the occupational structure. For example, figures from the U.S. Department of Labor show some of the estimated changes in the 1960–70 decade.

---

[17] Dugald S. Arbuckle, *Pupil Personnel Services in American Schools* (Boston: Allyn and Bacon, 1962) p. 16.

TABLE 1

ESTIMATED CHANGE IN EMPLOYMENT 1960–1970*

Occupation	Percent of Change
Professional and technical	+41
Proprietors and managers	+24
Clerical and sales	+27
Skilled workers	+24
Semiskilled workers	+18
Service workers	+25
Unskilled workers	0
Farmers and farm workers	−17

* U.S. Department of Labor, *Manpower: Challenge of the 1960's*, Washington, D.C.: (U.S. Government Printing Office, 1960).

While these are estimated changes, some rather definite trends can be seen. For example, by far the greatest growth will be in the professional and technical occupations. Considerable growth will also take place in the managerial, sales, and clerical occupations. The proportion of unskilled workers will decrease, probably, as a result of automation. The percentage of the labor force engaged in agriculture probably will continue to decline, again as a result of mechanization.

What is significant here is that those jobs requiring the lowest level of education are on the decline while those requiring a high level of education continue to increase. As this trend continues it may become almost impossible for an individual who has not graduated from high school to find a job. In short, for children in the elementary school today, a longer period of formal education will be necessary for most jobs.

It is also obvious that the speed of occupational change may necessitate an individual's changing jobs a number of times. As jobs disappear or as machines take over tasks formerly performed by men, individuals may find it necessary to retrain for a new job.[18] Career planning in the elementary grades, therefore, should focus upon developing positive and realistic attitudes about work and workers rather than upon a narrow area of specialization. To be an effective and contributing member of the new society, with the possibility of several careers for one individual, and with the necessity for continuing education, flexibility will be a must. Counseling services, beginning in the elementary grades, can provide the information and the understanding which will enable the child to make necessary adaptations and to enjoy change instead of fearing it.

X-Wed.

[18] Stewart and Warnath, *op. cit.*, p. 80.

Inner City and Outer City

Nature of the Problem

The growth of megalopolis during the past 50 years has produced vast social and economic changes in America. The steady move to the suburbs by white middle-class families has resulted in both racial and economic segregation in the inner city. These conditions have far-reaching consequences for the public schools.

Havighurst discusses some of the problems of metropolitan growth. First, it has led to increased segregation. This segregation is a threat to democratic unity and to educational opportunity. Second, space in the city is not properly used. The distance from residential areas to places of work, centers of leisure, and cultural activity is so great that many city facilities are not used and consequently not supported. These problems have had serious repercussions in education. The net effect has been to make the educational system less efficient and less effective in achieving its democratic goals.[19]

The Survey Research Center of the University of Michigan studied family incomes in Detroit and surrounding suburbs for the period 1951–59. This group found that income was directly related to the distance the family lived from the central city. Families living within six miles of the central business district had a median increase of only 3 percent during the eight-year period, while the cost of living rose 12 percent. Families living beyond the six-mile radius, or in the outer sections of the city, had an increase of 5 percent. During the same period, families living in the Detroit suburbs had an increase of 37 percent in income.[20] Several interpretations and explanations can be made here; however, the fact is that there is a wide social and economic difference between the inner city and the outer city. These differences produce opportunity and educational gaps which have far-reaching implications for society.

The problems of poverty and its effects upon children and youth is now apparent. In a 1967 statement on the *Welfare of Children,* President Johnson summarized these problems as follows:

> During these years of unparalleled prosperity, five and one-half million children under six, and nine million more under 17, live in families too poor to feed and house them adequately.
>
> This year, one million children, or one in every four, will be born to mothers who receive little or no obstetric care.

---

[19] Robert J. Havighurst, "Metropolitan Development and the Educational System," in Henry Passow, Miriam L. Goldberg, and Abraham J. Tannenbaum (eds.), *Education of the Disadvantaged* (New York: Holt, Rinehart & Winston, Inc., 1967), p. 20.

[20] Survey Research Center, "Family Income in Greater Detroit, 1951–1959," Ann Arbor, Mich.: The University of Michigan, 1960.

More than four million children will suffer physical handicaps and another two million will fall victim to preventable accidents or disease.

One million young Americans, most of them from poor families, will drop out of school this year—many to join the unhappy legion of the unemployed.

One in every six young men under 18 will be taken to juvenile court for at least one offense this year.[21]

Education

The problem of providing meaningful education for children in the inner city is complicated by several factors. Many are children of in-migrant parents, reared in the South and in Appalachia, and whose mode of life was drastically different. Others are from broken one-parent homes. Incomes are low, housing is poor, and opportunities are few. Many are on welfare.

The social and economic turmoil created by such conditions makes it difficult for children to understand the world around them and themselves in relationship to it. Further, such social and economic chaos often produces resentment and self-denegation, inhibits motivation, and in general leads to the development of negative attitudes toward school, the self, and toward society.

The way in which poverty and social class influence children in school is well documented. By every measure, children from low-income homes do not fare as well as children from more affluent families.[22] Goldberg describes some of the differences between lower and middle-income families as they relate to education.

Perhaps the most significant area of difference between lower and middle-class school populations relate to their differences in motivation toward school and their perceptions of the purposes and meaning of schooling. Miller and Swanson contrasted the values of the two groups as follows: The middle-class family members believe that their economic position can be improved through effort and sacrifice. They are willing to postpone gratification for greater future reward. They need to maintain a reputation for honesty, responsibility, and respectability. They must accumulate money and social graces, develop abstract thinking ability needed for advancement in their work. . . .

The middle-class child is "good" because from the earliest years he

21 President's Message to Congress, *Welfare of Children,* House of Representatives, Document No. 54, 90th Cong., 1st sess., February, 1967.

22 For detailed treatment of this topic, see Bernard Goldstein, *Low Income Youth in Urban Areas* (New York: Holt, Rinehart & Winston, Inc., 1967).

has been taught to control expressions of anger and to inhibit direct aggression. . . . He has learned that one cannot transgress against social demands if one wants to "get ahead." The lower class child has been brought up on direct expression of aggression in the home and in the street. Since control of such behavior is seen to have little relevance to social position or job maintenance, there is little need to teach the child the skills of control.[23]

Goldstein writes that social class background has a major impact upon the child's ability to learn to read. He cites Milner on this point.

Specifically, the lower class child . . . seems to lack chiefly two things upon entering school as compared with the middle-class child: a warm positive family atmosphere or adult relationship pattern which is more and more being recognized as a motivational prerequisite for any kind of adult controlled learning, not only of the verbal skills; and extensive opportunity to interact verbally with adults of high personal value to the child and who possess adequate speech patterns.[24]

While the sources of many problems of inner city children appear first in the home and in the community, some problems also appear in the school. Within recent years, schools have made some progress in such areas as revised methods of teaching, experimentation, and in developing intervention programs to help children overcome the adverse effects of their environment. However, many approaches to the educational problems of urban children and youth have been largely ineffective. Some have been ill-conceived, poorly timed, and inadequately financed. Many have failed to consider the disharmony between the schools' standards and expectations and those of the child. Coleman proposes the following new approaches to the education of the disadvantaged:

1. For those children whose family and neighborhood are educationally disadvantaged, it is important to replace the family environment as much as possible with an educational environment—by starting school at an earlier age, and by having a school which begins very early in the day and ends very late.
2. It is important to reduce the social and racial homogeneity of the school environment, so that those agents of education that do show some effectiveness—teachers and other students—are not mere replicas of the student himself. In the present or-

[23] Miriam L. Goldberg, "Factors Affecting Educational Attainment in Depressed Urban Areas," in Henry Passow (ed.), *Education in Depressed Areas* (New York: Bureau of Publications, Teachers College, Columbia University, 1963), p. 80.

[24] Goldstein, *op. cit.*, p. 35.

ganization of schools, it is the neighborhood school that most insures such homogeneity.

3. The educational program of the school must be made more effective than it is at present. The weakness of this program is apparent in its inability to overcome initial differences. It is hard to believe that we are so inept in educating our young that we can do no more than leave young adults in the same relative competitive positions we found them in as children.[25]

The changes recommended by Coleman may be a case of treating symptoms rather than causes. While changes in the school program and organization are probably long overdue, it is doubtful whether such changes alone would solve the educational problems in urban areas. Put another way, changes in education alone are not sufficient. A massive societal attack upon all the conditions that create problems for the inner city child should be planned and implemented.

Intensive Guidance Necessary

Expanded programs of guidance and counseling, beginning in the elementary grades, will be necessary if we are to deal effectively with the multiple problems in inner city schools. The need is so widespread and critical, however, that the usual complement of services and the traditional approach to guidance is not sufficient. Counselors must find ways to work not only with pupils themselves, but with teachers, parents, and the community. It is not enough to simply work on long-range objectives; the slum area child has some immediate needs that must be met if education is to have any meaning for him. Further, some educational objectives may not be relevant for many inner city children. It is therefore necessary to find ways to fit the school program to the condition and needs of students.

Tannenbaum believes that intensive guidance services are necessary if the child in a depressed area is to receive the personal and individual attention he needs. He feels, however, that the counselor-pupil ratio must be kept to a minimum if we are to get the job done. In the words of Tannenbaum: "There is simply too much to be done with insufficient personnel and the only solution is to augment these services either at school or in community agencies."[26]

---

25 James D. Coleman, "Equal Schools or Equal Students?" in Jeffrey K. Hadden, Louis H. Masotti, and Calvin J. Larson (eds.), *Metropolis in Crisis* (Itasca, Ill.: F. E. Peacock Publishers, Inc., 1967), pp. 290–96.

26 Abraham J. Tannenbaum, "Dropout or Diploma: A Socioeducational Analysis of Early Withdrawal," in Henry Passow, Miriam L. Goldberg and Abraham J. Tannenbaum, eds.), *Education of the Disadvantaged* (New York: Holt, Rinehart & Winston, Inc., 1967), p. 431.

One approach to guidance and counseling for inner city children and youth has been developed in Detroit under the direction of Dr. George E. Leonard of Wayne State University. The *Developmental Career Guidance Project* now operating in 12 inner city schools, elementary through senior high, places major emphasis upon working with children, teachers, parents, and the community in changing pupils' perceptions of themselves, their attitudes toward both school and their future. In addition to direct counseling with students, teachers are given help in understanding the special problems and needs of disadvantaged children and in developing guidance practices for use in the classroom. The services of counselors and paraprofessionals are also extended to parents who are given help in understanding the educational program and their child's participation in it. Nonschool personnel, such as business and community leaders, workers from various occupations, and parents are used extensively in a consultant and resource role and in supplementing the regular guidance program.

While all children require guidance and counseling services, the child from inner city has some unique needs that require special attention. The first requirement is to reshape our attitudes regarding what is relevant for children and youth in depressed areas. Second, educational changes designed to reduce the distance between school and life must be introduced. This is not a job for the counselor alone. However, because of his access to students, he ought to have first-hand knowledge of some of the problems and conditions that need attention.

The counselor in the inner city elementary school, in addition to spending a good deal of time with students, will also find it necessary to give major attention to working with teachers and parents in bringing about greater understanding of children and in developing closer ties between the school and the home. Involvement of community agencies and nonschool personnel in the guidance program is essential. Services from such agencies can be a major factor in motivation and can help to fill the void in the backgrounds of many inner city students.

Children and youth in the inner city are often unable to see the relationship between education and their future. They are typically poorly motivated, have poor self-concepts, lacking in understanding of future opportunities, and have low-level vocational aspirations. Massive programs of intervention carried on in the school and in the community are necessary to offset these conditions. The most strategic starting point is in the elementary school and key roles ought to be played by elementary school counselors.

Implications for Counseling

Turning now to the broad implications of societal influences for counseling in the elementary school, an earlier point should be reemphasized. Counselors must acquire a widespread awareness of influences outside the school which affect the behavior of children.

The emergence of elementary school guidance and counseling parallels our efforts to develop new approaches to education and to reorganize for more effective education for all children. The future promises more sweeping changes in our thinking about what is relevant, about the goals of education, and about practices and special services in the schools. The elementary school counselor will be asked to assume new responsibilities in effecting these changes. He may be expected to become the "validating agent"[27] for what is appropriate and necessary for students in a changing and complex society.

Corwin suggests that the schools of the future will become more specialized and that some teachers will be hired to work only with the gifted and others to teach such groups as the poorly motivated.[28] There is, of course, much evidence that such specialization has already developed both in instruction and in counseling. A large number of elementary school counselors have already been assigned to work in deprived areas, in special motivation programs, and in career development projects. These conditions have numerous implications for the counseling profession and may require some modification of our conceptions about the purposes of counseling in the school. For if the school becomes firmly dedicated to the notion that standard curricula, services, and resources are not sufficient in the present age, and if the idea persists that major emphasis must be given to such groups as the deprived, the gifted, and the unmotivated, then the role of the counselor will most certainly change. In such a specialized setting, the counselor who is committed to working primarily with the "average" student will find himself out of step with the times.

More specialization will require more counselors, since it is generally agreed that a lower pupil-counselor ratio is necessary in programs for students having special needs and problems. Different skills and understandings will also be required for those providing services to special groups.

While the counselor can make some definite contributions to the

---

27 See Ronald G. Corwin, *A Sociology of Education* (New York: Appleton-Century-Crofts, 1965), p. 201.

28 *Ibid.* p. 144.

educational and personal development of all types of pupils, under present conditions he can hardly be expected to be the expert and the consultant on every type of program in the school. Hopefully, new emphases in education will be accompanied by the recognition that several specialists with different backgrounds and skills are necessary to serve the diverse needs of students in today's schools. The counselor would then become a member of a team whose function is to provide direct assistance to students and consultative services to teachers and parents. The counselor would be the team member concerned chiefly with guidance.

Summary

What a child is and what he becomes is greatly influenced by the society in which he is reared. As society becomes more complex and as change accelerates the individual is constantly faced with a new set of conditions. He must cope with these new and changing conditions with a reasonable degree of success if he is to be a competent and effective member of that society.

One major type of assistance which the counselor can provide is to help children develop the ability to cope with change, and to acquire the self-understanding necessary to make adaptations to a changing world. One of the major requirements for the counselor is to know the setting in which he and his counselees operate. Up-to-date information on the trends in a dynamic society is a necessity.

The counselor's task in helping children achieve a place in society is not an easy one. In many cases standards, values, and conditions are changing so rapidly that other adults responsible for children are unaware of present and predicted changes. The counselor must, therefore, exercise some caution in assisting children in areas that are unfamiliar and even unpopular with adults. He will, therefore, need constant communication with his colleagues as well as with parents.

Selected References

BRONFENBRENNER, URIE. "The Split Level American Family," *Saturday Review*, October 7, 1967, p. 60.

COLEMAN, JAMES D. "Equal Schools or Equal Students?" in Jeffrey K. Hadden, Louis H. Masotti and Calvin J. Larson (eds.), *Metropolis in Crisis* (Itasca, Ill.: F. E. Peacock Publishers, Inc., 1967), pp. 290–96.

ERIKSON, ERIK. *Childhood and Society*. 2d ed.; New York: W. W. Norton & Co., Inc., 1963.

GOLDBERG, MIRIAM L. "Factors Affecting Educational Attainment in Depressed Urban Areas," in Henry Passow (ed.), *Education in Depressed Areas* (New York: Bureau of Publications, Teachers College, Columbia University, 1963), p. 80.

HAVIGHURST, ROBERT J. "Metropolitan Development and the Educational System," in Henry Passow, Miriam L. Goldberg, and Abraham J. Tannenbaum (eds.), *Education of the Disadvantaged* (New York: Holt, Rinehart & Winston, Inc., 1967), p. 20.

MICHAEL, DONALD M. *Your Child and the World of Tomorrow.* Washington, D.C.: National Education Association, 1966.

President's Message to Congress, *Welfare of Children,* House of Representatives, Document No. 54, 90th Cong., 1st sess., February, 1967.

STEWART, LAWRENCE H., and WARNATH, CHARLES F. *The Counselor and Society.* Boston: Houghton Mifflin Co., 1965.

TANNENBAUM, ABRAHAM J. "Dropout or Diploma: A Socioeducational Analysis of Early Withdrawal," in Henry Passow, Miriam L. Goldberg and Abraham J. Tannenbaum (eds.), *Education of the Disadvantaged* (New York: Holt, Rinehart & Winston, Inc. 1967), p. 431.

WRENN, C. GILBERT. *The Counselor in a Changing World.* Washington, D.C.: American Personnel and Guidance Association, 1962.

Chapter 4

Needs, Motivation and Learning

IN THE PREVIOUS CHAPTER IT was noted that the achievement of one developmental task paves the way for future developmental learnings. Each major developmental task is also related to a developing need. Thus a task such as learning proper social behavior is part of the process of satisfying the need for peer approval.

Cronbach has defined a need as follows:

> A need is a broad motive that makes certain types of goals important and attractive to the individual. . . . If John insists on his own way whenever he serves on a committee, he may need to prove that he is grown up and intelligent.[1]

In a discussion of the "Persisting Needs of Youth," Wrenn has stated that "children need security, affection, and meaningful activity. They need an understanding of the limitations with which they find security. They need chances for exercising the imagination and opportunities for feelings of achievement."[2]

[1] Lee Cronbach, *Educational Psychology* (New York: Harcourt, Brace & World, Inc., 1963), p. 112.

[2] C. Gilbert Wrenn, *The Counselor in a Changing World* (Washington, D.C.: American Personnel and Guidance Association, 1962), p. 4.

Whatever the needs of the child may be, school personnel, and especially the counselor, must be aware of them and efforts must be made to help the child satisfy these needs. This then, is the rationale for a chapter on the needs of children in a book on counseling.

The Needs Construct

According to Maslow, needs can be hierarchically arranged and grouped into two categories: biological and psychological. Within the category of biological needs, Maslow refers to (1) the *physical needs* for food, water, shelter, etc., and (2) the *needs* for safety, security, and freedom from anxiety. In the category of psychological needs, he refers to (1) the need for belongingness and love, (2) the esteem *needs* such as achievement, mastery competence, and the esteem of others. In regard to the esteem needs, Maslow writes: "Discontent and restlessness will develop unless the individual is doing what he is fitted for. What a man *can* be, he *must* be. This we call *self-actualization*."

Two additional categories of needs are described as (3) the need to know and to understand, and (4) aesthetic needs. In this hierarchy, the range is from the most potent survival needs such as hunger and thirst, up the scale toward higher needs such as needs for belongingness and love, cognitive needs, and needs for self-actualization. The lower level needs are more demanding and until they are reasonably well satisfied they have little influence on behavior. Thus a hungry or insecure individual whose confidence has been undermined by failure and frustration, will not be able to reach the level of self-actualization.[3]

Following Maslow's theory, when a child's basic needs are satisfied he does not have to be pressed or prodded into constructive work in school. The opportunity to become self-actualizing offers its own intrinsic rewards. When a child loses interest in class, rebels against study, and resists school, he may be tied up in an attempt to satisfy some lower level need, or he may not be getting sufficient opportunities to become self-actualizing. It is only through the satisfaction of these basic needs that the child's energies can be released for constructive and creative work.

Murray has also used the needs construct to describe behavior. His *primary* or *viscerogenic* needs include hunger, thirst, and others based upon the organic requirements for physical survival. The *secondary* or *psychogenic* needs are independent of organic processes

[3] Abraham H. Maslow, *Motivation and Personality* (New York: Harper & Bros., Publishers, 1954).

and include needs for achievement, recognition, acquisition, and others. Some needs can be dominant or, perhaps, can become dominant with changes in the situation. For example, one can develop a strong need to achieve if achievement leads to a desired recognition or reward. Murray recognized the hierarchy of needs but pointed out that this hierarchy can change with changing conditions.[4]

Mouly[5] also refers to physiological and psychological needs. His physiological needs include food, water, sleep, and rest, while psychological needs include the need for love, for belonging, for recognition, and for esteem.

Rogers has incorporated certain aspects of the needs theory into his explanations of behavior. He recognizes a number of specific needs, but there is one basic motive, that is to *maintain,* to *enhance,* and to *actualize* the self.[6]

As noted above, needs and motives are closely related. Jordan writes: "In general we think of a motive as a state of an individual which disposes him for a certain behavior and for seeking certain goals. Needs are much more general."[7] With this definition we turn now to a discussion of certain psychological needs as they relate to learning in the school.

Learning

Let it be understood from this point on at least, that the present author has no intention of presenting a lengthy treatise on the phenomenon called learning. The learning process is far too complex to be wrapped up in a brief chapter of a book on counseling. The reader who desires detailed information on learning and the learning process is advised to secure some of the many excellent books dealing specifically with this topic. There are two reasons, however, why it is appropriate to discuss learning in a general way and to draw some implication for guidance and counseling. First, the counselor is interested in all aspects of a child's development and it is the learning process which makes significant contributions toward development. Second, the literature in guidance and counseling has often placed little emphasis upon the child as a learner even though most counselors work in an institution that has learning as its main

4 Henry A. Murray, *Explorations in Personality* (New York: Oxford University Press, 1938).

5 George J. Mouly, *Psychology for Effective Teaching* (New York: Holt, Rinehart & Winston, Inc., 1960), pp. 24–25.

6 Carl Rogers, *Client-Centered Therapy* (Boston: Houghton Mifflin Co., 1951).

7 A. N. Jordan, *Educational Psychology* (New York: Henry Holt & Co., 1959), p. 205.

function. With this explanation then, let us proceed with a brief discussion of learning and its relevance for counseling.

Learning involves motive-incentive conditions such as the general need for achievement or accomplishment. Learning is an episode in which a motivated individual attempts to adapt his behavior so as to succeed in a situation which he perceives as leading to a goal. Learning represents change and adjustment, and it has many concomitant effects.[8] In general terms then, learning takes place when the learner has wants, interests, and unsatisfied needs.

Motivation and Learning

The needs that are probably most important in school as sources of proper motivation or of troublesome behavior are needs for affection, peer approval, adult approval, independence, competence and self-respect. Cronbach has described these needs as follows:

1. Need for Affection. Close affectional ties with a few persons provide the chief satisfactions for most people. The home and the family are the major forces in fulfilling this need. Work, recreational, and creative activities are secondary.

While achievement within itself can be satisfying, most people find greater pleasure in appreciation from family and friends. When these close ties within the family are absent, most people work out acceptable substitutes for these warm relationships. The child who is deprived of affection in the home may find affection in a teacher. Adults may find their substitute in a career or in community service.

2. Need for Approval by Peers. Each child learns early that getting along with others of his own age is pleasurable and that their disapproval is unpleasant. For pleasure and comfort in relations with others he must feel that he "belongs." Popularity with one's peers is an aid to development and learning. The child who is popular can learn more easily because he can be more creative without the fear of ridicule from others. The child who feels socially secure converts schoolwork into a social activity, while the child who feels rejected tends to work alone.

3. Need for Approval by Authority. The child doing what his teachers or parents expect, or the adult keeping on the good side of his boss are all concerned with approval from authority figures. In growing up there will be some conflict between the desires of the child and the restrictions of adults. Consistent and predictable

---

[8] Sidney L. Pressey, Francis P. Robinson, and John E. Horrocks, *Psychology in Education* (New York: Harper & Bros., Publisher, 1959), pp. 247–58.

responses from adults will more nearly lead to a wholesome resolution of this conflict.

4. NEED FOR INDEPENDENCE. The requirement that one becomes more independent through making his own decisions and doing things on his own is to some degree in conflict with training for obedience. Independence requires that a person express his own will while at the same time maintaining a balance of control.

The young child first experiences independence through exploration. If his choice of objects to clutch brings criticism he may learn that acts of independence cause trouble. The child who is not criticized or frightened into undue dependence will develop interests of his own and will find satisfaction in his own activities.

5. NEED FOR COMPETENCE AND SELF-RESPECT. One of the most important needs in terms of motivation for learning is concerned with attitudes toward the self in relation to the external world. The happy competent person is committed to goals, active in his approach to life, and generally optimistic. The defective personality on the other hand is often plagued by feelings of uselessness and inadequacy.

The need for competence as an element in learning and healthy adjustment cannot be overemphasized.

Cronbach writes:

As the child approaches school age and is given more tasks to perform, the motivation to explore and master things for their own sake becomes overlaid with ideas of duty and approval. . . . Favorable responses from others do much to direct energies into useful channels. Being labeled a failure instills a sense of unworthiness that eliminates trying.[9]

We have been attempting here to emphasize the development of the "whole child" and the needs theory is only one way to describe that development. The above list of needs is not exhaustive; however, they represent basic understanding for the counselor and the teacher.

Fransden has developed a set of motive-incentive appeals which provides specific ways of motivating children and youth in the school. His inventory includes the following.

1. *Curiosity*—the desire to understand one's world and oneself.

2. *Mastery*—achieved by adjusting learning tasks in every cur-

[9] Cronbach, *op. cit.,* p. 125–26.

riculum area to the individual's level of maturity and pattern of abilities.

3. *Knowledge of progress*—revealed by a frequent check on "how I am doing."

4. *A sense of self-enhancement*—the feelings that one's potentialities or capabilities are recognized and utilized. Self-enhancement is dependent on knowledge of progress.

5. *Love and affection from the teacher*—identification with a loved and admired person, and a sense of belonging and being accepted by the teacher.

6. *Praise or approval*—from both teachers and classmates.

7. *Opportunity to win special privileges*—such as going to the library for free reading or winning a contest.

8. *Feelings of security*—about one's status with respect to achievement, grade promotion, and social and affectional relationships.[10]

Table 2 illustrates some of the processes involved in satisfying the needs for affection, approval, independence, and competence. The ages given in the table are only averages. Children develop and learn at different rates; thus behavorial differences can also be expected to occur at different ages.

Conditions of Learning

Jordan refers to three general conditions of learning: physiological, psychological, and educational. Physiological conditions refer to the state of health of the individual such as visual, auditory, coordination, and the general health of the individual. Psychological conditions include motive, drive, interest, ego-involvement, and level of aspiration. The educational conditions having a most positive influence upon learning are described as: (1) goal-directed learning, (2) pupil involvement in planning learning activitites, (3) relating what is learned to real life, and (4) frequent evaluation of progress.[11]

There are several aspects of learning which have been disregarded in this chapter but which are nevertheless important. For example, the physiological needs have not been discussed in detail but it should be obvious that a hungry child or a sick child will not learn.

---

[10] Arden N. Fransden, *Educational Psychology* (New York: McGraw-Hill Book Co., 1961), p. 216–17.

[11] Jordan, *op. cit.*, p. 265–66.

TABLE 2

THE SATISFACTION OF NEEDS*

Stage	*Physical Characteristics*	*Need for Affection*	*Need for Approval by Adults*	*Need for Approval by Peers*	*Need for Independence*	*Need for Competence and Esteem*
Infancy (birth–18 mos.)	Crawls by 9–10 mos., toddles by 15 mos.	Learns to trust adults. Learns feeding and sleeping schedule				Seeks out and grasps objects within reach
Early Childhood (ages 2–5)	Walking and talking usually by age 2	Forms a secure identification with like sex parent	Learns to accept adult rules. Accepts denial of wishes, begins to understand restrictions	Learns about the rights of others. Knows "his" and "mine." Learns to share	Accepts separation from parents for short periods. Expresses own wishes through requests	Begins to learn some control of environment. Strives to develop some physical and cognitive competency
Middle Childhood (ages 6–9)	More even growth. Physical equilibrium	Generally strives to please parents and school authorities	Develops some emotional control. Accepts rules of the teacher and the school	Learns play skills, strives for group acceptance	Makes more decisions on his own. Begins creative activity at a higher level	Begins mastery of school work. Developing physical skill. Learns game rules
Late Childhood (ages 10–12)	Growth spurts. More physical disequilibrium		Makes an effort to be understanding and accepting of rules. Strives for achievement	Accepts group standards. Conforms to sex role	Works without being told and without supervision	Develops higher level interests, has his own projects, finds means to get some material possessions on his own

* Adapted from Lee J. Cronbach, *Educational Psychology*, New York: Harcourt Brace & World, Inc., 1963.

Other conditions such as readiness, level of aspiration, the selection of materials to be used, teaching approach, and teacher attitude are all direct influences on learning.

IMPLICATIONS FOR COUNSELING

The elementary school child of today is growing up in a highly complex and rapidly changing society.

The demands which that society makes on its members are more numerous and complex than a generation ago. In short, for full participation in society, one is supposed to know more, to be more productive, more involved, to relate better to others, and to be more successful than ever before. He is expected to be more stable and more competent than his forbears. At the same time he is confronted with more ambiguities, more problems, and less security, than ever before. The home, the church, and the neighborhood no longer provide the experiences and the opportunities necessary to develop the attitudes and competencies necessary for adequate functioning in a complex society. Many children grow up in an atmosphere of insecurity and mistrust with little opportunity to satisfy needs that contribute to a fully functioning person. More and more the school, by necessity, has been attempting to fill this void and help children to overcome the adverse psychological effects of nonschool experiences, or more appropriately, lack of experiences. Again and again, we have described the role of the school and the counselor in meeting the needs of children and youth. To emphasize this point further we quote from Willey and Andrew, the list of needs of youth which are of major concern to the counselor.

1. *Ethical and Moral Living: independence of action;* emancipation from parents; normal relationships with the opposite sex.
2. *Citizenship:* a satisfying place among fellow men; *status* with peer group, social and civic *competency*.
3. *Self-Realization: achievement;* use of leisure; achievement of emotional security. All youth need some degree of success and a feeling of accomplishment.
4. *Health:* All children and youth need to develop and maintain good health and physical fitness.
5. *Tools of Learning:* All youth need to have a command of the tools of learning such as reading, listening, thinking, and expressing thoughts clearly.

6. *Work Experience and Vocational Competency:* All children and youth need to acquire those understandings, attitudes, and skills necessary to plan an occupational future in line with one's capacities and interests.[12]

The counselor must understand not only the needs of the child; he must understand also the sources of those needs. Tolbert writes:

Of particular importance to the counselor is the source of needs, drives, and motives. Why does it make a difference to the pupil if he gets in the right classroom? It is a learned or secondary drive, rather than a primary need such as the need for food or water. The learned or secondary needs have their origin in the satisfaction of primary needs in social situations, for example, in the home. The approval of others, being associated with the gratification of psychological needs, becomes in itself need-reducing. In the same way, the individual can learn to need the approval of others.[13]

SUMMARY

The needs of children which have particular relevance for the elementary school counselor include: competence, independence, approval and acceptance. Of these, the need for acceptance is of primary importance. Acceptance includes feeling important and wanted by both the peer and adult society. In an age when many children have little or no opportunity to contribute and to participate in family and community life, it becomes difficult for the child to view himself as a valued and important member of society. It then becomes the responsibility of the school to see to it that the child becomes a valued and participating member of the school society.

If the counseling service in the elementary school is to meet the needs of children and help them to become competent and participating members of society it becomes tremendously important to understand what these needs are. Further, it should be noted that needs and motives are in a constant state of change. As the child grows, and as he masters one developmental task and moves on to the next, his needs also change.

Maximum development of the individual is the aim of any effective counseling program.

The focus in such a program is upon the developmental needs of

---

[12] Roy DeVerl Willey and Dean C. Andrew, *Modern Methods and Techniques in Guidance* (New York: Harper & Bros., Publishers, 1955), pp. 116–17.

[13] E. L. Tolbert, *Introduction to Counseling* (New York: McGraw-Hill Book Co., 1959), p. 161.

children. The counselor may find some of the concepts discussed in this chapter relevant to his work with children. However, in order to develop the competence necessary for assisting children and youth to become truly self-actualizing, the counselor is advised to explore far beyond the boundaries imposed by this chapter.

Selected References

FRANSDEN, ARDEN N. *Educational Psychology*. New York: McGraw-Hill Book Co., 1961.

MASLOW, ABRAHAM H. *Motivation and Personality*. New York: Harper & Bros., Publishers, 1954.

MOULY, GEORGE J. *Psychology for Effective Teaching*. New York: Holt, Rinehart & Winston, Inc., 1960.

MURRAY, HENRY A. *Explorations in Personality*. New York: Oxford University Press, 1938.

ROGERS, CARL. *Client-Centered Therapy*. Boston: Houghton Mifflin Co., 1951.

WILLEY, ROY DEVERL, and ANDREW, DEAN C. *Modern Methods and Techniques in Guidance*. New York: Harper & Bros., Publishers, 1955.

PART III

Counseling

THE COUNSELING FUNCTION has probably elicited more discussion than any other single topic in elementary school guidance. Much of this discussion centers around the unique factors in counseling with children and upon the necessity for making some adaptations in techniques when counseling with children in the school setting. Articles by Peters (1959), Dinkmeyer (1966), Nelson (1966), and Aubrey (1967) have provided some helpful suggestions and stimulated further discussion on this topic.

Counseling is the essence of the guidance function. It contributes in a more direct way to the realization of the goals of guidance than any other activity. The elementary school counselor who fails to recognize that counseling pupils is the major reason for his existence will lose his identity as a counselor. He may then become a coordinator, an assistant administrator, or school troubleshooter. In the meantime, the fundamental needs of children go unmet.

There are several questions relating to the specific process of counseling with children that still need attention. However, there are some areas of general agreement that have implications for the elementary school counselor. Part III describes some of the processes and techniques that seem most appropriate for counseling in the elementary school setting.

Chapter 5, dealing with child study, stems from the author's assumption that reliable and current knowledge about a pupil's developmental status is necessary for effective counseling. Some test and nontest approaches to child study are described.

Counseling the individual pupil is treated in Chapter 6. Some of the assumptions underlying this chapter are as follows:

1. Counseling can affect positive behavioral modifications in elementary school children and such modifications carry over into new situations.

2. Children can verbalize their concerns during counseling and do initiate counseling topics, particularly those relating to the self and interpersonal relations. There are some differences between lower and upper grade elementary children in terms of the child's verbal capacity and level of maturity necessary to work on a problem.

3. Counselors in the elementary school tend to assume more responsibility for the conduct of the counseling interview than do counselors of adolescents or adults. The degree of counselor responsibility assumption is related to cognitive factors and to the child's reasoning capacity. While the higher degree of counselor responsibility is often necessary and appropriate, this does not mean that the child cannot and should not make his own decisions. It does suggest some possible changes in our traditional thinking about counselor behavior during counseling.

4. Communication is a most important factor in counseling interviews with children. The language of the child is qualitatively different from that of the adolescent. Communication breaks down if the counselor relies solely on verbal dialogue and if the counselor interprets a child's language as he would that of an adolescent (Aubrey, 1967).[1]

5. Elementary school children, particularly at lower grade levels, are not sufficiently mature for major problem solving and long-range

---

[1] Roger F. Aubrey, "The Legitimacy of Elementary School Counseling: Some Unresolved Issues and Conflicts," *Personnel and Guidance Journal,* Vol. 46 (December, 1967), p. 356.

planning. The counselor, therefore, must always consider the developmental status of the child.

Chapter 7 deals with counseling children in groups. While group counseling is a controversial topic, it is a technique that holds much promise for working with some elementary school children. However, just as in individual counseling, some modifications of the usual group techniques are necessary when working with children.

Chapter 5

Child Study in Counseling

In the previous three chapters, an attempt was made to describe the child and to identify some of the influences on total development. This overview of developmental processes, needs, and learning, should provide the student or the counselor with a broad understanding of children and their concerns, and thus suggest several implications for counseling in the elementary school. The purpose of this chapter is to describe some procedures and techniques that can be used in understanding each pupil as an individual and as a learner.

The efficiency of the counseling service in the elementary school is dependent upon information concerning (1) the developmental status of the pupil, and (2) the influence of the home, the school, and the community upon pupil behavior and adjustment. The gathering and utilization of information about pupil potentialities, needs, and characteristics is a vital consideration in attempting to help pupils develop personal competency.

The child in the elementary school is a growing, developing, and changing individual. New situations and new tasks are constantly confronting him. The child cannot make the decisions and adaptations necessary to successfully meet these new situations unless he understands himself. Neither can the counselor help children to understand themselves nor to evaluate their status unless the counselor fully understands each child.

Willey emphasizes the need for understanding all aspects of pupil growth in the following statement:

> At the risk of encouraging an atomistic approach to child study, we can recognize four areas of pupil growth; physical, emotional, social, and intellectual. Total growth is recognized as an integration of all areas; and although each area may be subjected to special consideration and analysis, we cannot realize progress without reference to the other three. The child grows through constant interaction between himself and his environment; thus, to understand him thoroughly we need data concerning his personal needs, and the needs of the society in which he lives.[1]

To emphasize an earlier point, counselor understanding of pupils in and of itself is not sufficient. The ultimate aim is to help the pupil understand himself. Through self-understanding, the pupil can set goals and make plans and decisions necessary to total development.

Appraising Developmental Status

One approach to understanding the child is through an appraisal of his developmental status. Using the developmental task concept the counselor can identify and diagnose developmental problems. Five areas which require consideration by the counselor are described below.

Developmental Readiness

We have previously noted that all children go through approximately the same developmental stages. However, they do not progress from one stage to the next at the same rate. Each child is a unique individual. He may be the same age and have the same height and weight as his peers but his readiness for learning tasks may deviate significantly from his age group. The negative consequences of forcing a task upon a child before he is ready for it may endure throughout his school years. When children are confronted with tasks beyond their level of maturity they tend to become discouraged and to lose interest. In addition they are likely to develop negative attitudes toward school, toward teachers, and toward themselves. Some children, however, are able to master some tasks much

---

[1] Roy DeVerl Willey, *Guidance in Elementary Education* (rev. ed.; New York: Harper & Bros., 1960), p. 63.

earlier than their age mates. Children with advanced maturity may also lose interest and develop negative attitudes if the mastery of significant developmental tasks is postponed too long. Some assessment of the child's developmental readiness—intellectual, emotional, and physical—is vital to the process of setting goals for learning, and to the counselor's function of aiding significant others in understanding the child.

Achievement Status

Developing fundamental skills in reading, writing, and arithmetic is a major task of middle childhood.[2] Assisting students to master these tasks is the primary objective of the elementary school. Knowledge of the child's scholastic achievement as well as data on general intelligence, special abilities, interests, and problem-solving ability is basic to counselor or teacher understanding of the pupil. School achievement is, of course, related to social and physiological influences and it would be misleading to diagnose problems solely on the basis of academic achievement.

The appraisal of academic achievement alone is not sufficient. The entire developmental pattern of the child must be considered; that is, achievement in such areas as social learning, physical status, and capacity for independent planning must also be considered. In making a diagnosis of the child's achievement status, the counselor will need to rely upon data from school records, tests, and interviews, as well as upon information from teacher and parent consultation.

Attitudes toward the Self

The influence of the self-concept on the behavior of the growing child is discussed in two other sections of this book and thus does not require detailed treatment here. It is important to emphasize, however, that this aspect of a child's developmental status must receive careful attention if an accurate appraisal is to be made.

Again, one of the basic tasks of development is the establishment by the individual of his own identity as a separate being with a will of his own. Much of this process takes place during the school years. It is to this aspect of development that school experiences may make one of its most significant contributions.

As Redl and Wattenberg point out, one of the purposes behind the school's evaluation program should be to help children develop a realistic self-image. It should be recognized, however, that children cannot be bluntly forced to recognize that they are "dumb" or

---

[2] Robert Havighurst, *Developmental Tasks and Education* (New York: Longmans, Green & Co., 1962).

unattractive. This does not mean that youngsters must remain completely blind to the weaker aspects of their personality. In fact, some youngsters accept the fact that they have some weak points as well as strengths in certain areas. If a child's self-image is too far below his ego ideal, he is quite likely to be discouraged or defensive.[3] An accurate picture of the self-image can assist the counselor and teacher to understand many of the child's reactions.

Social Development Status

The child is an interdependent social being. Much of what he is and what he will become is influenced by his relationships with others.

Much social development takes place during the preschool years. Children learn habits of sharing, cooperation, and taking turns as they play with other children during the first few years of life. In school, social development continues and takes on added significance. On the one hand, they must learn to accommodate themselves to the patterns required in the school, and on the other they must learn to adjust to conflicts and to handle crises resulting from interaction with a larger group of age mates and adults. A fundamental task at this period is learning to relate to others and learning to live with the human relationships they develop. Success in social living is basic to learning. The counselor must not only understand the child's attitudes toward social demands, and his attitudes toward peers and adults, but he must also understand how the child is developing in such areas as self-responsibility, self-control, and self-confidence.

Coping with Crises

Life's stages and developmental tasks both present some problems and some conflicts for the individual. To cite Erikson, a child does not become an adolescent nor does an adolescent become an adult without conflict—a matter which Erikson gives developmental status and describes as *crisis*. He writes; "To each such unity corresponds a major crisis; and whenever, for whatever reason, a later crisis is severe, earlier crises are reviewed."[4]

At every age level, children have to deal with some problems and some conflicts. The process of growing up involves constant change in relationships both at home and at school. The expectations and

---

[3] Fritz Redl and William Wattenberg, *Mental Hygiene in Teaching* (2d ed.; New York: Harcourt, Brace & World, Inc., 1959), p. 120.

[4] Erik Erikson, *Insight and Responsibility* (New York: The W. W. Norton & Co., Inc., 1964), p. 138.

the requirements which the culture holds for the child also changes at each stage of development.

The most important change in the young child's life comes when he enters school. Here he meets a new set of standards and requirements. The tasks required by the school may clearly represent crises. During the first few months of school, the child experiences elements of both freedom and restriction and encounters both success and failure. He is beginning to develop a style of coping with these new problems and this coping behavior can be either appropriate or inappropriate. The task of the counselor is to understand this coping behavior and to assist the child to develop patterns of dealing with conflicts that are in harmony with his maturity.

The above constructs are interrelated and overlapping. It is thus inappropriate to appraise pupil status without consideration of all the above elements. The constructs do seem helpful to the counselor in that they serve as guideposts for the establishment of meaningful contacts with counselees and they also provide the counselor with some measure of the counselee's level of functioning. Such understanding is necessary in deciding upon the most appropriate plan for helping the counselee.

Technique for Appraising Developmental Status

From a consideration of critical areas of development, we turn now to a discussion of some of the tools and techniques for appraising developmental status. The list of pupil appraisal techniques discussed in this section is not exhaustive. The purpose of this section is to describe some of the approaches to pupil appraisal or individual inventory that seem appropriate for the counseling service. Further, it is not suggested that the counselor alone is responsible for pupil appraisal. Appraisal is a function of all school staff members—teachers, counselors, psychologists, and administrators. The counselor utilizes data from many sources so that he will be more able to understand and help the pupil. He is most concerned with information that will highlight the individuality of the counselee. Data gathered through the use of the techniques described below are particularly helpful to the counselor in his analysis of the individual.

Observation

Observation is a foundational technique in guidance. Every other technique and tool used in the guidance of pupils is an extension of our basic ability to observe. We can increase our skill in understanding pupils by refining our ability to observe clearly and objectively. Peters, Shertzer, and Van Hoose describe observation as follows:

Observation requires exquisite discernment and alert perceptions to the events around us. Observation is concerned with that which is considered normal as well as that which deviates from the standards of behavior one might expect in a given situation. Observation gives us cues; observation helps to arouse us to make an analysis of the behavior of pupils during a formulation of hypotheses which may be proven or disproven by additional observations. The greater the number of observations done with a purpose, the more extensive are the possible meanings and usefulness of these observations.[5]

Observation yields facts which may refute certain hypotheses and confirm others. It provides deeper insight into the dynamics that shape the child's behavior and development. It is a practical way of testing the hypotheses that have been made about a pupil. Most important, it provides a means for evaluating the effectiveness of the steps that are being taken to facilitate his learning, his development, and his adjustment.[6]

Observation provides insight and information on pupils which cannot be obtained by other techniques. The different reactions of pupils in similar situations are important indicators. The expressions on faces, differences in posture, and the manner of talking all provides clues. Adults have learned to smile at the remark, "It wasn't what he said, it was the way he said it." There is even greater wisdom in observing how children act. It is not only what they do, but the way they do it that can speak volumes to the careful observer. A dramatic illustration of this point is provided by the film *Balloons,* produced by the Child Study Department at Vassar College. In the film two boys are seen hitting balloons. One strikes them with tense gestures and clenched fists. The second boy hits with smooth, confident motions. The differences in behavior are interpreted to mean that the first boy has strong destructive impulses, while the second boy has no such conflicts.[7]

Purposeful observation requires skill and objectivity on the part of the observer. Bias in observing and reporting pupil behavior may result from the observer's feelings and values and also from lack of skill in focusing on what is really significant. Accurate observation

---

[5] Herman J. Peters, Bruce Shertzer, and William H. Van Hoose, *Guidance in Elementary Schools* (Chicago: Rand McNally & Co., 1965), p. 87.

[6] Daniel A. Prescott, *The Child in the Educative Process* (New York: McGraw-Hill Book Co., 1957), p. 212.

[7] Redl and Wattenberg, *op. cit.,* pp. 36–37.

requires the ability to evaluate objectively what is happening as well as an awareness of one's own feelings about observed behavior.

Redl makes the following suggestions on things to observe about children:

Attitudes toward Adults. Does he act toward adults realistically? Does he try to "pull a fast one" or show that he likes or dislikes you? How long does your influence over him last?

Attitudes toward Other Kids. How well does he get along? Who are his friends and enemies and on what basis? How do the others react to him? How popular, ignored, or rejected is he? How ready to share, defensive, or suspicious is he?

Group Role and Attitudes toward the Total Group. Is he liable to assume or desire any one of the following group roles: leader, second-in-command, clown, teacher's pet, bully, isolationist, ring-leader, model boy, scapegoat, organizer? How does he act to group pressure, group acceptance, or group rejection? Does he show any group pride, group ambition, or group feeling?

Attitudes toward Routine and Discipline. What daily functions go most smoothly with him? How does he respond to routines? Does he accept control and restrictions?

Interests and Aversions. What does he like best and least? How does he satisfy his interests? What are his main aversions and areas of avoidance? How constant or changeable are his interests?

Special Strong Points. What are his strong points and finest assets? What special skills does he have? In what areas of life does he function most normally and healthily, at least if given a chance?

Problem Trends Revealed. What are his main difficulties, the weak points in his organization, his areas of greatest confusion and most inadequate functioning? Under what conditions are these weaknesses more emphasized or more in the background?[8]

Shertzer and Stone offer the following guidelines for accurate observation.

1. Before observation takes place, determine what is to be observed. The purpose of observation should be known in advance. What dimensions of behavior are to be investigated? Knowing these things will add meaning and purpose to observation.
2. Observe only one pupil at a time. Few well-trained observers can watch with any degree of accuracy more than one person at a time. When group behavior is studied, film and recording

[8] Fritz Redl, *When We Deal with Children* (New York: The Free Press, 1966), pp. 333–337.

equipment should be used to obtain a record of the multitude of happenings that takes place simultaneously.

3. Watch for significant behavior. Just what is significant may not be known at the time, just as many of the things a pupil does are trivial and reveal nothing about him.

4. Spread observations over the school day. Time samplings for brief periods of time often reveal a truer description of his behavior than a description obtained from a few prolonged observations.

5. Learn to observe without resorting to note writing during the observation period. The presence of a pad and pencil often cues children regarding what is occurring and results in behavior different from what might be obtained if these were absent.

6. If possible, record and summarize the observation immediately after it is taken.[9]

Anecdotal Records

A report of observed behavior is recorded in the anecdotal record. The anecdote is a statement of the incidents of behavior that take place during the normal course of events and that are singled out as being significant in depicting developmental status. A single incident, taken alone, may have no particular significance; it becomes important only when related to other incidents observed over a period of time.

The anecdotal record can provide the counselor with vital information for individual analysis and in addition can be an aid in helping the counselee understand himself. The student must understand himself if satisfactory progress and adjustments are to be made. Quite often the objectivity of elementary school students in looking at themselves leaves much to be desired. Therefore, the counselor must often help the pupil to see how he is reacting in a variety of situations. The anecdotal record, reporting exactly the behavior observed, can be a valuable aid in this process.

An individual's behavior is a response to his needs for acceptance, security, affection, and competence, and a way of dealing with conflicts, threats, and frustration. The sensitive counselor or teacher will record and interpret anecdotes within this framework. Teachers are in a most strategic position to observe and report on behavior, and counselors, by virtue of their understanding of development processes, are in a position to interpret the significance of pupil behavior both for the pupil and for the teacher.

Traxler's discussion of the value and use of anecdotal records is helpful here. The following ideas are particularly noteworthy:

---

[9] Bruce Shertzer and Shelley Stone, *Fundamentals of Guidance* (Boston: Houghton Mifflin Co., 1966), p. 229.

1. Anecdotal records provide a basis for recording descriptions concerning the behavior of pupils in a variety of situations. They afford a means toward understanding the core or basic personality pattern of each individual and of changes in the pattern.

2. They provide a means whereby the attention of the teacher or counselor can focus on the individual pupil.

3. They encourage an understanding of the larger school problem through analysis of behavior in both formal and informal settings.

4. They provide information of particular value to the counselor in understanding individual pupil needs and in planning help for the pupil.[10]

Rating Scales

Rating scales have considerable value as a means of learning about children. Having other persons in the school describe characteristics of children can provide the counselor with insights into behavior not possible to obtain from other sources.

Rating scales are of three types: descriptive, numerical, and graphic. In the descriptive rating scale, provision is made for a list of descriptive phrases from which the rater selects the one most applicable to the pupil rated. This form of scale is illustrated as follows:[11]

A. Descriptive Rating Scale
Directions: Place a check mark in the space before the phrase which describes this pupil.

_____ Is sensitive to the feelings of others.
_____ Accepts suggestions and help.
_____ Enjoys group work.
_____ Can be counted upon to do his part.
_____ Respects the property of others.

In the numerical rating scale, only numbers are assigned to each trait. The following example illustrates this scale.

B. Numerical Rating Scale
Directions: Describe the pupil from 0–10 to represent the degree to which he possesses the traits listed. 0 represents none, 5 an average amount, and 10 a maximum amount of this trait.

_____ Cooperative.
_____ Eager worker.
_____ Indolent.
_____ Leadership.

---

10 Arthur E. Traxler, *Techniques of Guidance* (New York: Harper & Row, Publishers, 1957), p. 132.

11 Adapted from Willey, *op. cit.*, pp. 80–81.

The graphic rating scale, shown below, is the scale most frequently used and is the best known of the rating scales. In this scale the units or degrees are placed on a continuum, with descriptive phrases placed under the line.

C. Graphic Rating Scale

Directions: Describe this pupil by placing a check at the point which best describes the degree of the trait which applies.

Distracted: Jumps from one thing to another	Difficult to keep at a task until completed	Attends adequately	Absorbed in the task	Able to hold attention for a long period

Rating scales have both advantages and limitations that should be understood. The advantages most often cited are that they are a means for quantifying observations and that they provide for several different ratings of the same individual. Like other instruments, rating scales are also subject to error. Among these errors are personal bias, the halo effect, and errors of judgment. Further, teachers are more apt to be consistent in rating such traits as scholarship, alertness, and cooperation, than in rating such things as sensitivity, leadership, and interest. The problems surrounding the intelligent use of rating scales should be carefully analyzed so that the scales do not prove a negative factor in helping children.

Self-Reports

Self-reports may take the form of questionnaires, personal inventories, self-rating scales or sentence completion tests. They are forms or devices used to help children describe or evaluate themselves. It should be understood that we are not discussing the projective devices generally used by the clinician, even though data gained through the use of such techniques may prove helpful to the counselor. Some self-reports are a form of projection or semiprojection and as such can reveal something about the child's personality structure and his inner world.

A. Sentence Completion Tests. Sentence completion is one of the oldest forms of self-description and can be most useful in contributing relevant information on several facets of personality. It has several advantages over the direct question approach in that it helps to divert the attention of the child from himself and thus may help him to divulge feelings of which he is unaware.[12] The most common form of the sentence completion test presents the beginning of a sentence, and the child is asked to write anything he wishes to complete the sentence.

Science Research Associates report upon the use of this technique with a group of sixth-grade pupils. Their set of incomplete sentences included the following:

1. I'm proud of myself because..........................
2. My best work in school is............................
3. I could improve myself by............................
4. I wish my classmates would...........................
5. I would help my class by.............................
6. The kind of friend I like best is....................
7. I wish my parents would..............................
8. I wish ....[13]

Some sample items that are frequently found in other sentence completion tests include:

1. My greatest worry is.................................
2. People think that I..................................
3. I often ....
4. My goals ....
5. I like ....

Among advantages listed for the incomplete sentence tests are (1) it reveals some general patterns of behavior; (2) aids in understanding the individual's feelings; (3) assists the child in self-understanding; and (4) aids teachers and counselors in drawing some conclusions about pupil attitudes.

This technique should not be used to measure "good" and "poor" adjustment of students nor should it be assumed that children always reveal their true feelings through the incomplete sentences technique. It is only one measure of personality and if it is to have any significance must be carefully analyzed and interpreted. Further, data from incomplete sentences must be supported by evidence gained from other sources.

B. Storytelling Methods. Entire books have been written on the theme of studying an individual through analysis of his oral and written expression. No attempt is made here to provide the prospective counselor with the clinical sophistication necessary to assess per-

---

[12] *Ibid.*, p. 125.

[13] Science Research Associates, *Special Guidance Report* (Chicago, 1962).

sonality from an analysis of written or oral composition. The nature of the counseling function in the elementary school does not lend itself to unrestricted use of such clinical procedures, and furthermore, the reliability and validity of such methods is questionable.

The essence of our discussion here is that it is possible to gain some understanding of the child through his written and oral expression. The key to the use of such methods is in the counselor's ability to interpret what is said or written. Furthermore such methods are not used alone; they are merely one more way to understanding pupils.

For many young children it is essential that expression be oral. The technique of having the child tell a popular story, or tell the story he likes best is sometimes used. Children's interests in comic-strip characters have also been used with some success. In this technique, children can be asked to describe what is happening or to talk about the characters.

Children who have learned how to write can be asked to write a story, or to give a written explanation of "What I Like Best," or "What I Would Like to Be." Permitting the child to write about anything he chooses can also provide some helpful information. By reading or listening to children's stories it is possible to gain some knowledge of their concerns, their interests, and their wishes.

The major advantages of such techniques are in the opportunities that the child has for spontaneity of expression and for producing something that is important to him. The major disadvantages lie in the fact that such methods may reveal nothing or they may be colored by the immediate situation. Further children's expressions are difficult to evaluate, and almost always reflect the ability of the child to describe what he thinks, sees, or feels.

When used properly, children's stories can provide some measure of attitudes, feelings, and concerns. Such methods are treated here because they may offer some ideas on different approaches to studying children.

The Interview

The counseling interview is discussed in some detail in Chapter 6. In this section, however, it is appropriate to emphasize that the person-to-person relationship of counselor and pupil during the interview is a most satisfactory way of gathering information about the child.

The interview is particularly useful because of its flexibility, and the possibility of pursuing main points of concern and for checking the accuracy of information from other sources. It also provides an opportunity for pupils to express themselves freely concerning activities, interests, anxieties, and plans.[14]

A common language is essential for the conduct of the interview. Problems arise when the counselor and child are communicating on different levels and when they are using different language. Children often do not have the maturity necessary for understanding what the counselor is saying. Here is where the ability and the flexibility of the counselor is put to a real test. It is the counselor who will have to make the adaptation, not the counselee. The use of a vocabulary that is understood by the counselee is essential. This is illustrated in the following exchange between a counselor and a fourth-grade pupil.

COUNSELOR: "Then how did you feel?"

COUNSELEE: "Oh, I felt fine, but it still made me mad."

Or in the conversation between a counselor and a sixth grader.

COUNSELOR: "Well, uh, I'm not sure, but we could explore that area if you would like?"

COUNSELEE: "Uh, we could what?"

In counseling with children it is often necessary to recast words or phrases into simple terms that the counselee can easily understand. Many children, even in the upper grades, may not grasp the meaning of certain words or phrases commonly used by counselors, even when they appear to be clearly stated. It then becomes necessary for the counselor to interpret, to rephrase, and to check the counselee's understanding of what is said.

In interviews with children, the use of psychological terms and high-sounding phrases are unnecessary. The use of down-to-earth terms and simple words will produce best results in interviewing.

TESTING IN COUNSELING

Historically, testing has always been closely associated with guidance. Moreover, child study in schools has placed heavy emphasis upon testing in diagnosing and predicting behavior. The routine in dealing with children on an individual basis has been to subject them to a battery of tests. When a child is suspected of having a really serious problem the school psychologist is called in to administer the *Binet,* the *WISC,* the *Draw-a-Person,* the *Wide Range Achievement* or anything else that happens to be in his black kit. Too often, not much attention is given to talking the matter over with the child or his parents. This sudden and unexplained barrage of testing by a total stranger often arouses the youngster's suspicion and anxiety to a point that the test results may be totally invalid.

---

[14] Traxler, *op. cit.,* p. 32.

Group tests of achievement and intelligence, while most generally administered to all children in certain grades, have also been widely mismanaged and misused. Again, the emphasis in group testing has been upon evaluating the pupil's weaknesses. The pupil is more often viewed as a recipient of testing and his participation is most generally involuntary.

The purposes of testing should be consistent with the purposes of elementary school guidance. Properly used, tests can be helpful in appraising the developmental status of pupils and in aiding the pupil in self-understanding. Further, the school-testing program in the school should provide for the evaluation of all pupils, not just those with problems.

It is assumed here that the counselor will not be the overseer of testing in his building; rather that he will use test results in his work with individuals and with groups of children. The use of tests in diagnosis and counseling are described below.

Appraising Developmental Status

In order to properly understand and assist the pupil, some measure of his developmental status is necessary. When used in concert with other pupil data, test results can provide the counselor with valuable information on general ability, achievement, and readiness. Data from tests administered as a part of the school's testing program can be helpful in identifying special talents and weaknesses of a pupil and can aid the counselor in deciding upon the most appropriate type of intervention. In some cases results of individual tests, administered by a school psychologist, may also be useful in appraising the pupil's developmental status.

It should be emphasized that giving or using tests in counseling is no more indicative of a diagnostic attitude than is making any other kind of observation or inference. Tests are simply one more device for gaining some information about the individual.[15]

Pupil Self-Understanding

The use of tests as an aid in developing pupil self-understanding appears to have considerable potential. Leonard's study of third and sixth graders investigated the questions of (1) whether elementary school students can grasp the concept of individual differences and (2) whether elementary school students can apply this concept to themselves. His experiment included having pupils rate themselves before testing, and again after tests were interpreted to them. The

[15] Donald H. Blocher, *Developmental Counseling* (New York: The Ronald Press Co., 1966), p. 133.

results indicated that pupil self-estimates moved closer to reality after a discussion of their test results. He concluded that many elementary school pupils do not have an accurate picture of themselves and that test interpretation can be a useful technique in aiding pupils in self-understanding.[16]

The counseling use of tests focuses upon pupil self-study and decision making. While tests generally used in school cannot be expected to contribute to self-understanding in all areas of development, they can aid the pupil in understanding his learning potential, his achievement status, and his special interests and aptitudes. They can aid children in setting goals and in developing realistic plans for themselves.

Interpreting Test Results

The usefulness of tests in counseling or consultation depends in large measure upon how skillfully the test is interpreted. Test interpretation requires a thorough understanding of the specific test as well as its implications for the person involved. The counselee's question "What does this mean for me?" must be dealt with. In the case of test interpretation for teachers and parents, care must be taken to ensure that they understand the significance of the test for their work or their relationship with the child. The following principles are involved in test interpretation for counseling and consultation purposes.

1. Interpretation of tests requires at least minimal understanding of measurement principles.
2. The test interpreter must be sensitive to the individual's feelings about tests and about himself.
3. Some preliminary explanation of what tests are, what they can do, and what they cannot do, as well as an explanation of the "why" of the specific test, should be provided.
4. The individual should understand that test scores are not absolute measures of behavior, and that they should be considered in relation to other information from nontest sources.
5. Use terms that can be understood. Some measurement and statistical terms are confusing to teachers and utterly meaningless to students or parents.
6. The individual must be given the time and opportunity to raise questions, to comment, and to react to what he has learned from test interpretation.

---

[16] George E. Leonard, "Utilizing Test Results in the Elementary Classroom," *The School Counselor,* October, 1964, pp. 3–5.

When a pupil receives information through test interpretation that is inconsistent with his estimate of himself, he may not readily accept the information that is provided. Careful explanations by the counselor to help the child understand that this is only one estimate of him, and acceptance of the child's feelings about the test can allay negative attitudes.

Blocher writes that an important consideration in test interpretation is that the test represents a tool to be used to facilitate some more important counseling goal. Test interpretation should be integrated into the context of the counseling interview in a way to ensure maximum meaning for the counselee.[17]

Summary

An adequate understanding of the pupil, his needs, his potentialities, and his developmental status is vital to counseling in the elementary school. To understand the pupil thoroughly, we need data on developmental readiness, achievement status, attitudes toward self, social development status, and coping behavior.

Several techniques have proven helpful in providing the counselor with some measure of a pupil's developmental status. The most revealing techniques for use with children include observation, teacher ratings, and self-reports. Standardized tests, when used properly, can also provide valuable information about pupils.

The counselor is interested in diagnosing pupil strengths and weaknesses in order to plan appropriately with the pupil. He is also concerned with the development of pupil self-understanding so that the pupil can learn to make his own plans and decisions. The approaches described in this chapter can be used in a counseling context to the end that both of these objectives are realized.

[17] Blocher, *op. cit.*, pp. 135–36.

Selected References

Erikson, Erik. *Insight and Responsibility.* New York: The W. W. Norton & Co., Inc., 1964.

Leonard, George E. "Utilizing Test Results in the Elementary Classroom," *The School Counselor,* October, 1964, pp. 3–5.

Peters, Herman J., Shertzer, Bruce, and Van Hoose, William H. *Guidance in Elementary Schools.* Chicago: Rand McNally & Co., 1965.

Prescott, Daniel A. *The Child in the Educative Process.* New York: McGraw-Hill Book Co., 1957.

Redl, Fritz, and Wattenberg, William. *Mental Hygiene in Teaching.* 2d ed., New York: Harcourt, Brace & World, Inc., 1959.

Willey, Roy DeVerl. *Guidance in Elementary Education.* rev. ed.; New York: Harper & Bros., 1960.

Chapter 6

Counseling the Individual

COUNSELING, AS THE TERM is used in this section, refers to counseling normal children in the elementary school setting. Normal children are those who can attend and profit from participation in the regular classroom. In counseling with normal children, major emphasis is placed upon the positive aspects of pupil functioning and upon the developmental needs of pupils. Counseling at this level is not remedial or therapeutic. The elementary school counselor does not seek to bring about major structural changes in personality. While some children may need therapeutic assistance, this service should come from a specialist other than the school counselor.

Goals of Developmental Counseling

There are certain goals which are basic to counseling at any level. Regardless of the age of the counselee, the counselor attempts to stimulate in him a feeling of more adequate personal adjustment on the one hand, and to increase his effectiveness in dealing with his environment on the other. These goals are fundamental to counseling in any situation.

Dinkmeyer writes that the central purpose of counseling children is to help the child:

> 1. To know himself, his assets and liabilities, and through this self-understanding to develop a better understanding of the relationships among his own abilities, interests, achievements and opportunities.
> 2. To develop self-acceptance, a sense of personal worth, a belief in one's competence, a trust in oneself and self-confidence; and to develop an accompanying trust and acceptance of others.
> 3. To develop methods of solving the developmental tasks of life with a resultant realistic approach to the tasks of life as met in the areas of work and interpersonal relations.
> 4. To develop the capacity to become self-directive and to acquire problem solving ability.
> 5. To develop responsibility for his choices and decisions.
> 6. To develop wholesome attitudes and concepts of self and others.[1]

The counselor in the elementary school needs to establish some specific purposes and objectives for working with children. The following objectives, while not exhaustive, are appropriate to our discussion here. Counseling in the elementary grades should focus upon the following areas:

1. *Aiding in Self-Understanding*. The development of self-understanding among children and youth cannot be left to chance. If young people are to become effective and contributing members of society they must understand who they are and what they are capable of becoming. There must be a trained and interested staff member who has primary responsibility for aiding children in the development of self-understanding and self-acceptance. This calls for an organized guidance program and the services of an elementary school counselor. The counselor may assist children directly, however, he may also provide indirect assistance through working with teachers, parents and other significant adults in the child's life.
2. *Developing a Healthy Self-Concept*. The self-concept develops in accordance with the way a person perceives his experiences: his failures and his successes. His behavior and his performance tend to be consistent with his self-concept. The child learns to think and feel about himself as defined by others. In

[1] Don Dinkmeyer, "Counseling Theory and Practice in The Elementary School," *Elementary School Guidance and Counseling*, Vol. 1, No. 3 (June, 1967), pp. 196–207.

the development of a healthy personality, it is essential that the child make proper interpretations of his experiences in order that his self-concept contain realistic and unprejudiced elements. The task of the counselor is to understand the type of self-concept a child is developing and try to make sure that it will be both realistic and favorable enough that the child will be able to accept himself.

3. *Attaining Appropriate Academic Development.* Counseling assists the child to explore his abilities and interests and to make maximum use of his potential. Counseling can assist the child in building on his strengths and working toward alleviating deficiencies in academic skills. The counselor provides a non-evaluative relationship and a non-threatening atmosphere in which the pupil can make an objective self-appraisal. The increased understanding of the academic self which the child develops through counseling can have a positive impact on classroom performance.

4. *Aiding Children with Vocational Development.* Students in the elementary grades need some help in gaining the relevant vocational knowledge that helps further the developmental process. Individual help on such matters as understanding one's talents, abilities and interests and learning how to utilize strengths is a long and complex process which should begin in the elementary school. In our competitive society we expect and, except in unusual cases, demand that each individual make some contribution. Work is essential, and if a person is to find his place in life he must be prepared to function as a worker. Elementary school children aided by the counselor can be helped to understand the importance of work and the effects of work upon their lives.

5. *Learning to Deal with Complex Interpersonal Relationships.* Through individual counseling, elementary pupils can learn how to approach more thoughtfully and skillfully the continual interpersonal relationships in which they are involved. They can learn the how and why of their attitudes and their reactions to the people in their lives. In the safe and facilitating atmosphere of counseling, they can explore their feelings about others. They can learn how to relate to their peers and to adults.

6. *Alleviating Personal and Emotional Problems.* Pupils in the elementary grades do have personal and emotional problems for which they need assistance. Problems such as shyness, lack of confidence, worrying, and problems in peer relationships often arise. Linder's[2] study reveals that many pupils having such prob-

[2] Edward Linder, "A Study of Selected Sixth Graders to Determine Where a Child Would Go for Guidance" (Unpublished Masters Essay), Ohio University, Athens, Ohio (1963).

> lems prefer the assistance of an elementary school counselor. The counselor, in helping pupils find ways to solve a single problem, may provide avenues to the solution of larger problems.

The developmental approach to counseling is predicated upon the belief that individuals are capable of progressively developing self-understanding, self-appraisal and self-direction.

Counseling and Developmental Tasks

Since the achievement of the developmental tasks is so crucial to adequate functioning and adjustment, it is vitally important that maximum opportunities and assistance in developmental task mastery be provided at an early age. Zaccaria suggests that the developmental task concept has several implications for counseling.[3] Byrne writes that counselors in the elementary school may serve the basic counseling function of the developmental check-up.[4] According to Havighurst, "A developmental task is a task which arises at or about a certain period in the life of the individual, successful achievement of which leads to his happiness and success with later tasks, while failure leads to unhappiness in the individual, disapproval by society, and difficulty with later tasks." For example, the tasks of walking and talking are usually achieved by the age of two, and the child who fails to achieve these tasks about this age may be handicapped in mastering future tasks. Likewise, the major tasks of middle childhood include the acquisition of fundamental skills in reading, writing and arithmetic. Accomplishing these tasks successfully paves the way for future development and learning, while failure to do so places the child at a serious disadvantage. Zaccaria emphasizes this point:

> The achievement of basic developmental tasks results in greater happiness and satisfaction for the individual. Success in mastering developmental tasks also leads to societal approval and a chain of other events which cumulatively enhance more adequate personality integration, more adequate personal development, and the mastery of the general developmental tasks of each life stage.[5]

---

[3] Joseph S. Zaccaria, "Developmental Tasks: Implications for the Goals of Guidance," *Personnel and Guidance Journal,* Vol. 44, No. 4 (December, 1965), pp. 372–375.

[4] Richard H. Byrne, *The School Counselor* (Boston: Houghton Mifflin Co., 1963), p. 124

[5] Zaccaria, *op. cit.*

Erikson's "critical stages of development" concept appears to be in general agreement with the above concepts.[6] The reader is referred to Chapter II for a detailed discussion of the Psychosocial Stages of Erikson. The thinking of both Havighurst and Erikson is important to our discussion here. They appear to be in general agreement with the following developmental task concepts relating to childhood:

1. Growth and development is a continuous process.
2. For descriptive purposes, growth and development can be divided into stages.
3. Most individuals in any culture pass through fairly well-defined stages of growth.
4. Each society makes rather definite demands upon its members.
5. These demands differ from stage to stage as the individual moves through the developmental process.
6. Developmental crises appear when the individual perceives the demand to alter his present behavior.
7. Meeting the crises successfully by mastering the required tasks leads to societal approval and success with later crises and tasks.
8. Failure to master the task or crisis leads to disapproval by society and difficulty with later crises and tasks.

The developmental task concept provides the student and the counselor with relatively discrete criteria for evaluating the student's developmental progress in many areas. Thus, developmental tasks may be viewed as stepping stones whereby the student, assisted by the counselor, can achieve the broad goal of personal competence.[7]

Table 1 contains a list of the developmental tasks of middle childhood (ages 6-12)[8] and shows the level of help provided by the elementary teacher and the elementary counselor in assisting children to master these developmental tasks. While teachers and counselors are not the only adults who assist the child in the successful or acceptable achievement of these tasks, both the counselor and the teacher can provide major help with those tasks most closely related to learning and living in the school.

---

[6] Erik H. Erikson, *Childhood and Society*, 2nd ed. (New York: W. W. Norton Co., 1963).

[7] Zaccaria *op. cit.* p. 375.

[8] Havighurst, *op. cit.*

TABLE 1

Developmental Tasks of Middle Childhood *
(Age 6–12)†

Levels of Help Given by Teacher and Counselor in Assisting Children with Developmental-Task Mastery	*Little* 1	2	*Some* 3	4	*Much* 5
1. Learning physical skills necessary for ordinary games	C	T	...	...	...
2. Building wholesome attitudes toward oneself as a growing organism	...	...	T	...	C
3. Learning to get along with age mates	...	...	...	T	C
4. Learning an appropriate masculine or feminine social role	...	...	T C	...	...
5. Developing fundamental skills in reading, writing, and calculating	C	...	...	...	T
6. Developing concepts necessary for everyday living	...	...	T	C	...
7. Developing conscience, morality, and a scale of values	...	...	T C	...	...
8. Achieving personal independence	...	...	T	...	C
9. Developing attitudes toward social groups and institutions	...	...	T C	...	...

* T = Teacher, C = Counselor.

The elementary teacher has a responsible role in assisting the child with developmental task mastery. Her chief concern, however, is the child as a learner, and the teacher focuses upon helping him acquire the basic skills in reading, writing, and arithmetic. Such comprehensive assistance cannot generally be provided by the classroom teacher alone. Thus, the teacher and the counselor may serve as cofunctionaries in evaluating and working on developmental task problems. It is through joint awareness, concern, and effort, that adequate development is reinforced and incipient developmental problems prevented.

The elementary school counselor is concerned with the pupil's total development. In addition to working with teachers the counselor assists children with developmental task mastery in several

† Havighurst, *op. cit.*

other ways. Through individual and small group counseling he assists children in learning who they are and what they are capable of becoming. In the nonthreatening climate of counseling, the child can learn to view himself realistically and to develop a positive attitude toward himself and the world around him. He can be helped to capitalize upon his strengths and to make the most of his educational experiences.

The growing child needs some assistance in developing healthy and meaningful relationships with peers and adults. The elementary school counselor can assist the child to understand his reactions to other people and the reactions and attitudes of other people to him. In the safe atmosphere of the counselor's office, children can explore and develop an understanding of their feelings toward others. The following segment of a counseling interview with a third-grade boy illustrates this point.

COUNSELOR: Uh, tell me how you're getting along with Joe and Ronnie now. Tell me about that.

PUPIL: Well, uh, ahh, they always tell me I'm a baby and I tell them to shut up.

COUNSELOR: Uh huh. You tell them to stop.

PUPIL: Yeah, and yesterday I told Miss —— about them talking while she was out to the, uh, out to the, ah, the room.

COUNSELOR: You told the teacher about them.

PUPIL: Yeah, and uh last night going home they threw my cap in the water. Then they laughed and ran. They both laughed. [Pause] And today I saw Ronnie with a book of matches, you know like, uh, like you use for, for lighting stoves and I told Miss —— on him, and she'll get him I bet. [Pause]

COUNSELOR: Uh, could you tell me why you think they pick on you? Ah, tell me what you think about it.

PUPIL: Uh, [pause] uh, they think they're big. They think they're smart.

COUNSELOR: Mm. I see. Maybe if you just stay away from them, uh, maybe, just don't bother with them, ahhh, do you think that would help?

PUPIL: Ah, uh, I don't like them anyway.

COUNSELOR: I see. Uh, maybe it would be better if you didn't tell the teacher about them. Do you think? [Long pause] Uh, you have some other friends. Maybe you could play with and be with them for awhile.

PUPIL: I like Terry and Art. We play all summer, and now too.

COUNSELOR: You are good friends.

PUPIL: Yeah.

COUNSELOR: Any other friends?

PUPIL: Uh, no, not now. Paul was my friend but now he isn't.

COUNSELOR: Uh, what caused that? [Pause] You and Paul, I mean.

PUPIL: He got mad, uh, he got mad because I wouldn't let him use my ball-point. He said I was a cry baby. Uh, [Pause].

COUNSELOR: Uh, huh. I see. Ah, sometimes we may want to share with our friends. Maybe we can try to be fair with them, uh, what do you think?

PUPIL: Uh, yeah, I guess.

COUNSELOR: Well let's plan to talk about this some more O.K.? Uh, maybe we can talk again soon and see what we can work out. O.K.?

In helping the child to understand and accept himself and his strengths and capabilities, the counselor is aiding the child in developing a basis for decision making and goal direction. As he learns to make decisions and to assume responsibility for his actions the child is gaining the experience necessary for achieving independence and for making the choices necessary to future progress and development. The following counseling interview with a sixth-grade pupil shows how the pupil moves in the direction of understanding his concerns and selecting alternatives.

PUPIL: And I didn't get home until almost 4 o'clock. After I played outside for awhile and ate I didn't have much time. So I practiced awhile and didn't get a chance to study.

COUNSELOR: You felt it was important to practice your music.

PUPIL: Yeah, well I have to go for my lesson tonight, and Miss —— she wants us to practice a lot. I mean I guess I have to do this and if I wouldn't, uh, I don't have much time.

COUNSELOR: You don't have enough time to keep up with your schoolwork and the piano too?

PUPIL: Uh, I have a lot of things to do, and ah, you know. My mom rented the new piano and uh I have this trumpet that I have played since the fourth grade and now I can play about any song, but I'm kinda tired of it. [Pause] Now my grades keep getting worse.

COUNSELOR: You think, uh, if you didn't have to practice piano you could do better work in school?

PUPIL: I want to do my best. I may take something else next year. I mean I don't want to be the best of everybody. I want the best grades I can.

COUNSELOR: Well, uh, as you know your mother called me after your last report card. I think she understands the situation and asked me to talk with you again. Uh, I think you can do better work, ah, your records and tests tell that you are a good student but maybe, ah, right now you can't do much better if you keep up with your piano lessons.

PUPIL: I need to get good grades, I don't want to fail, and there's a lot of new stuff in arithmetic. I want to spend more time. I could take piano again some other time.

Society expects certain levels of performance and behavior of every person. A person is judged in accordance with his willingness or ability to measure up to these expectations and is accepted or rejected on this basis.

Each year of his life a child is expected to accomplish certain developmental tasks. During the elementary grades the child is expected to learn certain basic skills, to get along with his age mates, and to begin to develop personal independence. Children need assistance in accomplishing these and other tasks if they are to meet the expectations of society. The elementary school counselor has a major responsibility for providing this assistance.

Special Considerations in Counseling with Children

Although counseling is recognized as a key activity in elementary school guidance, too little attention has been given to the specific processes of counseling children in the school setting. Research in this area has been quite limited and much of the literature has assumed a transfer of principles and procedures from secondary school counseling or from counseling in a clinical setting. Some progress appears to have been made in the past two years, however, and several points from recent research and literature will be discussed here.

In 1965, Van Hoose[9] analyzed 30 transcripts of counseling interviews with children in grades 1–6. He found that elementary school children are able to assume responsibility for counseling and to verbalize their feelings to a degree necessary for counseling through the use of interview techniques. However, it was found that the child does not generally have all the skills and understanding necessary to work on a problem or to develop and follow through on a plan of action. He concluded that the elementary school counselor must consider the relative immaturity of the child when counseling with him. This finding may suggest that the elementary school counselor will need to assume more responsibility for direct assistance to the child than does the counselor of adolescents or adults.

In a more recent study it was found that elementary school coun-

---

[9] William H. Van Hoose, "Dimensions of Counseling With Children." *Guidance Journal,* Vol. 5, No. 2 (Fall, 1966), pp. 83–88.

selors in actual interviews with children tend to help the child select or identify the topic or problem to be worked through. What appears to happen is that the child tends to express his concerns in a vague global sort of way and the counselor then finds it necessary to help him pinpoint his real concern. The conclusion to be drawn here seems to be that the child is not as verbal as the adolescent and that he does not generally have all the skills necessary for describing what really bothers him.[10]

Hawkins investigated the topics that elementary school children discuss in interviews with counselors. She found that the three topics most frequently discussed were related to home, school, and self. Hawkins reports that children in both the upper and lower elementary grades were able to verbalize in counseling interviews. Discussions in counseling involved both problems or concerns of the children and content that was not problem centered. She concluded that children in the upper elementary grades talk more and discuss a wider variety of topics during counseling than children in the lower grades. Another important finding from this study was that elementary school counselors as a group assumed greater responsibility than the children did for the initiation of topics discussed. However, topics such as self and interpersonal relations were initiated by the children with a frequency equal to that of the counselor.[11]

These findings seem to suggest that when counseling with children:

> 1. There are certain dependency factors which restrict the child from changing many things in his environment. The child's choices are, therefore, limited when compared with the adult's opportunity to manipulate his environment.
> 2. There is a need for greater sensitivity in working with non-verbal cues. The child is not as verbal as the adult, and the counselor must try to determine the deeper meanings of his words and expressions.
> 3. The child is not sufficiently mature for major problem solving. Cognitive factors in counseling are different than with the more mature individual and the counselor must always consider the child's reasoning capacity.
> 4. The elementary school is really involved in a re-educative process when working with children. He is working toward the development of self-understanding, the modification of behavior,

[10] Irene Mann, *In-Counseling Behavior of Children* (Master's Essay), Wayne State University, 1967.

[11] Sue Hawkins, "The Content of Elementary Counseling Interviews," *Elementary School Guidance and Counseling* Vol. 2, (December 1967), pp. 115–19.

and the development of increased social interest and awareness.
5. Both cognitively and emotionally, the elementary school pupil's perception of time is *now*. The counselor is thus required to deal with immediate matters and concerns in contrast to the counselor of adolescents who helps his clients focus upon the future.

The elementary counselors in Brooks[12] study reported that much of their counseling with children occurred outside the counseling office. Brooks states that elementary counselors interview children on the playground, in the library, in the hallway and in other areas where children study and play. This is understandable when we consider that both cognitively and emotionally children's perception of time is *now*. Thus, the need for immediate help is often crucial.

Dinkmeyer has written that counseling in the elementary school setting is vastly different from counseling children in the guidance clinic or in private practice. The nature of the counselee is different in that the counselor focuses upon the developmental problems of all students. Too, the counselor is part of a school team and must be aware of the educational objectives and practices of the school.[13]

The Counseling Process

Counseling in the elementary school may involve the counselor and child, counselor and teacher, or counselor and parent. This one-to-one service which the elementary school counselor provides requires that he possess certain skills acquired as a consequence of professional preparation, experience and capability. While some of the activities of the elementary school counselor may be quite similar to those of counselors in other settings, the emphasis and methods and techniques used by the counselor in the elementary school are significantly different.

The most obvious difference results from the nature of the elementary school pupil and the educational-social milieu in which he lives. As Peters[14] has pointed out, the organizational structure of the elementary school provides a teacher-pupil relationship which enables the teacher to assist the child with many of his concerns and

[12] Lois Brooks, *Duties of Elementary School Counselors* (Unpublished manuscript), Wayne State University, 1967.

[13] Don Dinkmeyer, *Toward A Theory of Child Counseling at The Elementary School Level* (Chronicle Guidance Publications, 1965).

[14] Herman J. Peters, "Differential Factors Between Elementary and Secondary School Counseling," *The School Counselor*, Vol. 7 (October, 1959), pp. 3–11.

problems. Too, there is a significantly greater dependency relationship involving the parents of elementary school children. The elementary school pupil makes fewer decisions on his own and is less future-oriented than the adolescent. The relative immaturity of the elementary school child and his inability to verbalize his concerns are additional factors that require modification of techniques when counseling with children.

Basically, there are four levels on which the counseling system in the elementary school functions to help children. These levels may be described as follows:

1. *Level I: Individual Counseling*—The child may be assisted through the one-to-one relationship. This is the most frequently used method for dealing with learning and adjustment problems in the school.
2. *Level II: Group Work*—The helping process at this level may involve members of the peer group in either group guidance or group counseling.
3. *Level III: Consultation*—Other significant adults, such as parents, teachers, or other pupil personnel workers may become involved in the helping process after consultation with the counselor.
4. *Level IV: Program Alteration*—Programs, activities, or services relating to the child may be brought to the foreground; altered, modified, or changed in such a way that the child is aided in more effective development.

It should be understood that the above steps are not hierarchically arranged nor do they stand as separate or distinct aspects of the counseling process. In fact, the counselor and the counselee may be involved in two or all of the above levels simultaneously. Helping children through the use of groups, through consultation with others, and by effecting modifications of the child's program, is discussed in separate chapters of this book. Several techniques which the counselor may use in individual work with children are described below.

1. *Appraising*. A pupil needs to have an understanding of himself consistent with his capacity to comprehend at his maturity level.
2. *Information-Giving*. Guidance information-giving is concerned primarily with answering current questions which the counselee has and with helping the pupil develop a positive attitude for later educational and career decisions.

3. *Encouraging.* The encouragement technique gives the child some confidence in himself and reflects the counselor's faith in the counselee. Encouraging means that the counselor recognizes and capitalizes on the child's strengths, assets, and interests.

4. *Analyzing.* Analyzing one's self for full development is the crux of developmental counseling. The counselor uses several procedures for assisting the child in analyzing his total life space.

5. *Interpreting.* Interpreting is the search for significance of what is found in self-exploration. Interpreting may also include using data from guidance tools to gain deeper understanding of the counselee.

6. *Clarifying.* Clarifying is the process within the interpreting function. It brings into sharp focus the behavior under consideration and its implications.

7. *Approving.* The child is still in a stage of development and often needs direct assistance in planning. Although the elementary school counselor does not select the path or the direction he has a responsibility to give approval to one or several possibilities for positive action.

8. *Reinforcing.* This technique refers to reinforcing the "good" that is derived out of other aspects of the counseling process.[15]

The Counseling Relationship

The elementary school counselor tries to develop an accepting nonjudgmental relationship with his counselees. Basic to the counseling relationship is a respect for the unique nature of the child. The child is not viewed as an object to be shaped according to the will of the adult; rather, he is a person with individual rights, dignity and integrity.

The counselor uses his understanding of children, of counseling dynamics, and of environmental influences to try to understand each counselee. He tries to help the child, his parents and his teachers understand the forces influencing behavior. At the same time he recognizes that counselee insight in and of itself is not sufficient and may not be necessary. As Ginott has pointed out, some children can change their behavior without a clear understanding of why they had problems.[16]

The counselor has several responsibilities in establishing an effective counseling relationship. Among his responsibilities are:

---

[15] The above material is based upon: H. Peters, B. Shertzer, and W. Van Hoose, *Guidance in The Elementary Schools* (Chicago: Rand-McNally, 1965).

[16] Haim G. Ginott, "Play Group Therapy: A Theoretical Framework" *International Journal of Group Psychotherapy VIII* (1958), p. 410.

1. To communicate to his counselees his commitment to them and his desire to help them.

2. To behave in such a way that children see him as a person they can go to for counseling.

3. To assist directly the child who has difficulty communicating his concerns or feelings. With some children this assistance with communication may be verbal or the counselor may need to use play media to help the child express himself.

In spite of some views to the contrary, there is now ample evidence that many elementary school children do voluntarily seek counseling help. Child-initiated counseling represents the apex in establishing an effective counseling relationship. In such cases the counselee recognizes the need for help and has reached a state of readiness to work on a problem. The counselor's task is to accept, to understand, and to help him more clearly identify and remove obstacles to adequate adjustment and performance.

It is also recognized that some children who have problems do not seek help on their own. In this situation it is possible that the child is not aware of his problem and its implications. Too, it is also possible that the child does not see the counselor as the type of person to whom he can turn for help. Assuming that such cases are referred by teachers or other adults, there are several procedures the counselor can use to establish a good counseling relationship. The first requirement is to let the child know that it is quite alright to seek help from an adult and that the counselor will assume major responsibility for providing that help. Too, the counselor must convey to the child the understanding that they can talk privately and that he will listen. The counselor must convey to the child some idea of what can happen in counseling including what the child can expect from the counselor.

The Counseling Interview

The interview can be an effective technique for counseling with children at the elementary level. The counseling interview can help the child understand certain cause and effect relationships, to make more desirable choices of behavior, and to solve specific problems. The use of the interview as a primary technique for counseling with children has been discussed by Yarrow.[17] He describes the interview as a technique particularly well suited to assessing a child's perceptions of the significant people in his environment.

[17] Leon J. Yarrow, "Interviewing Children" in Paul Mussen (ed.) *Handbook of Research Methods in Child Development* (New York: John Wiley and Sons, 1960), p. 569.

The interview can be a most effective method for counseling with normal children and can aid in greater understanding of the child as well as increase counselee self-understanding. However, if the counselor is to truly reach the child he must deal with concepts appropriate to the child's level of understanding. Further, the interview behavior of the counselor must be consonant with the counselee's interpretation of the relationship between himself and his environment.

Counseling interviews with children in the elementary grades present some special problems not usually encountered in counseling with adolescents or adults. One special problem is the motivational involvement of the counselee. The elementary child may not always enter counseling as a result of some intrinsic desire for help; often the motivation is extrinsic. Further, the child is accustomed to finding security with and direct assistance from adults, and may thus expect direct help from the counselor.

Communication is a critical factor in counseling with children. As mentioned elsewhere in this book, a common language is essential. While the counselor and the child may use the same terms, the child's understanding and interpretation of words or phrases may be very different from the counselor's meaning. Aubrey points out that the language of the child is qualitatively different from that of the adolescent, depending upon the age and prior experience of the individual. Techniques used with adolescents break down when dealing with children if one relies solely on verbal dialogue, or if the counselor makes the same interpretations of a child's language as he makes for an adolescent or adult.[18]

The counselor may find it necessary to check frequently on the child's use of words as well as the child's understanding of language used by the counselor. Both verbal content and feeling tone of the interview must be in harmony with the child's developmental adequacy.

The child is still in a dependent state. Maturationally and experientially he has a long way to go by comparison with adolescents. He cannot be expected to be wholly responsible for his actions. The elementary school counselor does not give the child the major responsibility for planning, for selecting between alternatives, and for making decisions. This means that the counselor must share with the counselee the responsibility for the conduct of the interview and

[18] Roger F. Aubrey, "The Legitimacy of Elementary School Counseling: Some Unresolved Issues and Conflicts," *Personnel and Guidance Journal,* Vol. 46 (December 1967), pp. 355–59.

for developing an approach to problem solving. The ultimate objective is counselee self-understanding, self-direction, and fulfillment.

The Life-Space Interview

The life-space interview is a technique used by Redl[19] in his work with disturbed children. However, it has many possibilities for counseling children in the school setting. The life-space interview occurs, whenever possible, in the same setting as the behavior that prompted the interview. The purpose of the life-space interview is to determine the child's reactions and interpretations of a particular experience as well as his feelings about a specific behavior. Since the world of the elementary child is often centered on the "here" and "now," dealing with immediate concerns and problems through the life-space interview is a valid approach in elementary school counseling.

To extend this idea, the elementary years are conscience, ego developing years. They are the years when children are incorporating their own controls, testing reality, and developing behaviors that enable them to cope with reality. The middle childhood years are extremely important in that children are attempting to find a balance between (1) The self-image, (2) The ideal, (what I'd like to be) and (3) Conscience (what I must not be). The life-space interview provides immediate help on problems inherent in growing up and also aids in self-understanding and self-evaluation.

Play Activity

There is still much discussion concerning play activity as a technique in elementary school counseling. Play activity with the normal child is an area still in need of much research. However, since it is not always a simple matter for the young child to "discuss" his problem with an adult some additional procedures must be used in an effort to adapt to the child's world of response. Play activity is one procedure that can be effectively used by the elementary school counselor. Nelson believes that it is "just as inappropriate to expect a young child to talk through his feelings as it is to expect an adult to use a sandbox or puppet."[20]

The elementary school child, and particularly the child in the primary grades is still at the stage where play is an important activity

---

19 Fritz Redl, *When We Deal with Children,* (New York: The Free Press, 1966), p. 35.

20 Richard Nelson, "The Use of Unstructured Play Media in Elementary School Counseling." *Personnel and Guidance Journal,* Vol. 45, No. 1 (September, 1966), pp. 24–27.

in his life. Play is an expression of the self. Through play, the child develops social roles, tests his concepts, and works through frustrations. In contrast to the child in the upper elementary grades who can and does verbalize his feelings, his fears, and his concerns, the young child *acts* these. Moustakas[21] points out: "He can express his anger and fear, be critical and resentful, carefree and joyous. In his play, he can carry out his imaginations and dreams, spontaneously and dramatically."

The elementary school counselor must utilize techniques which facilitate communication. Some elementary school children can be reached through play more readily than through a "talking" experience. It should be noted that some young children are perfectly capable of "discussing" their concern with an adult and many do just that.

Assuming then, that play activity is used as a counseling technique, how does the counselor apply this technique?

The actual techniques are not complex. However, the activity of the child must be carefully interpreted by the counselor. This requires competency in understanding the developmental needs, behavior, and motivation of children. The child's acts during play are merely a sample of behavior which requires careful analysis. Some of the meaning derived from play activity may be intertwined and complex. When the play gets into symbolic areas that suggest problems beyond the skills of the elementary school counselor, a referral should be made.

The role of the counselor beyond being alert to more complex problems and making referrals, also includes the understanding that a deep clinical analysis is not attempted. Since the counselor in the elementary school works mostly with "normal" children depth analysis is not usually necessary.

To paraphrase Nelson: The closer that statements relating to play behavior can relate to the actual behavior, the more they should be preferred. Statement number two should be preferred when a child suddenly and violently crumbles a piece of clay he has called his brother.

1. You really hate your brother so you smashed him.
2. You're angry so you crushed it.

The child may go on to verbalize feelings about his brother if that is in fact his concern. If the counselor is truly understanding him,

[21] Clark Moustakas, *Psychotherapy with Children* (New York: McGraw Book Co., 1958).

however, he will not need to go beyond the immediate behavior. In a real sense then, reflection in elementary school counseling through play activity, is preferable to analytical statements.

The incident described below may help to point up the value of play in elementary school counseling.

Doug was a bright second grader, referred to the counselor because of low grades and a negative attitude toward school. During the first interview he chatted informally with the counselor mainly about the telephone and the book shelf. He wandered about the room, sat on the floor, and picked up several objects, mainly for his own amusement. The first interview achieved little depth but did establish the beginnings of a counselee-counselor relationship.

In preparation for the second interview a week later, the counselor displayed several play objects including crayons, paper, and modeling clay. Almost immediately Doug selected a crayon and busied himself for several minutes drawing a bus. As the counselor discussed the drawing with the counselee, Doug described a recent experience from a long bus trip with his mother. The father had refused to accompany the family on the trip and considerable family friction had resulted.

In this incident play served as the medium through which meaningful communication could be established. Doug learned more than just play. He discovered that he was accepted and that he could express his feelings and anxieties without reservation.

This incident also illustrates another important aspect of a play experience, i.e. the child's relationship with the counselor. In this nonthreatening atmosphere in the presence of an understanding and accepting adult, the normal child can express whatever frustrations and resentments he may have. When he smashes the clay or slaps the doll he feels free to bring out whatever aggressive or hostile feelings he may wish. Play activity then, may be used as a type of preventive program of mental hygiene for normal children. Normal children can use play activity as a way of growing in self-acceptance and as a way of looking at attitudes that may not be easily explored in the classroom or at home.

Summary

The major objectives of counseling in the elementary school can be summarized as aiding children in (1) appropriate academic achievement, (2) furthering normal social and emotional development, (3) developing self-understanding, (4) acquiring realistic self-concepts, and (5) developing self-knowledge relative to the world of work. Counseling focuses upon the total individual in all aspects of development; the emphasis is therefore preventative and developmental, not remedial or therapeutic.

The elementary school counselor uses a variety of techniques in counseling children. The interview can be an appropriate method for counseling with most children; however, some modifications or variations of the interview technique may be required at the elementary level. Play activity may be appropriate with some children if the counselor has the understanding necessary to properly interpret the child's play.

Counseling is a professional task, requiring professional training and professional competency. Counseling is a key activity in guidance and contributes more directly to the attainment of guidance goals than any other service.

Selected References

DINKMEYER, DON. "Counseling Theory and Practice in The Elementary School," *Elementary School Guidance and Counseling,* Vol. 1, No. 3 (June, 1967), pp. 196–207.

HAVIGHURST, ROBERT J. *Developmental Task and Education* (New York: David McKay Co., Inc., 1952), p. 2.

HAWKINS, SUE. "The Content of Elementary Counseling Interviews," *Elementary School Guidance and Counseling,* Vol. 2 (December, 1967), pp. 115–119.

MOUSTAKAS, CLARK. *Psychotherapy With Children* (New York: McGraw Book Co., 1958).

NELSON, RICHARD. "The Use of Unstructured Play Media In Elementary School Counseling," *Personnel and Guidance Journal* (September, 1966).

PETERS, H., SHERTZER, B. and VAN HOOSE, W. *Guidance In The Elementary School* (Chicago: Rand-McNally, 1965).

VAN HOOSE, WILLIAM H., "Dimensions of Counseling with Children." *Guidance Journal,* 5:2 (Fall, 1966) pp. 83–88.

ZACCARIA, JOSEPH S. "Developmental Tasks: Implications for the Goals of Guidance," *Personnel and Guidance Journal* 44:4 (December, 1965) pp. 372–375.

Chapter 7

Counseling Children in Groups

GROUP COUNSELING has recently attracted considerable attention from counselors and other educators. This interest appears to be increasing as more attention is given to counseling children in the elementary school. Ohlsen has written that group counseling is an effective method for working with elementary school children, including those in the primary grades. He suggests, however, that several adaptations of general methods must be made when counseling with children.[1]

The rationale for group counseling stems from the assumption that many problems are primarily social or interpersonal, and that the individual's behavior is greatly influenced by group membership. The child benefits from group counseling through interacting with his peers, by observing their behavior, and by considering alternative behaviors. This process helps the child test his perceptions of himself, express his own feelings, and develop greater self-understanding.

[1] Merle M. Ohlsen, "Counseling Children in Groups," in Don Dinkmeyer (ed.), *Guidance and Counseling in the Elementary School* (New York: Holt, Rinehart & Winston, Inc., 1968), pp. 290–91.

Definitions

The distinctions between "group therapy," "group guidance," "multiple counseling," and "group counseling," are not always clear. Since counseling has generally been defined as a one-to-one process, the use of the word group is bothersome for some people and may thus require some redefinition of counseling. However, the term "group counseling," is an appropriate term for describing a kind of group activity and major objections to its use seem to have been satisfactorily answered.[2] Group counseling, as the term is used in this book, refers to what Shertzer and Stone describe as a "process in which one counselor is involved in a relationship with a number of counselees at the same time."[3] Knowledge of how each of the above terms are used in this chapter is necessary to effective communication, and thus require more precise definitions. The definitions given below are in harmony with the author's perspective of group work and may help to clarify several points made in this chapter.

Group Guidance

Group guidance is the term generally used to refer to guidance activities with more than one student. Group guidance traditionally involves the imparting of facts, the sharing of information,[4] or the group study of common problems.[5]

Group Therapy

Group therapy is usually defined as the application of therapeutic principles to two or more persons simultaneously. The term "therapy" suggests that the group leader is probably a clinical psychologist or psychiatrist.[6] Downing writes that the term "group therapy" belongs primarily to activity associated with psychotherapy. He feels that group therapy is usually for children with serious emotional problems.[7]

---

[2] Lester Downing, *Guidance and Counseling Services: An Introduction* (New York: McGraw-Hill Book Co., 1968), p. 223.

[3] Bruce Shertzer and Shelley Stone, *Fundamentals of Guidance* (Boston: Houghton Mifflin Co., 1966), p. 172.

[4] Walter Lifton, *Working with Groups* (New York: John Wiley & Sons, Inc., 1961), p. 11.

[5] Margaret Bennett, *Guidance and Counseling in Groups* (New York: McGraw-Hill Book Co., 1963), p. 9.

[6] Shertzer and Stone, *op. cit.,* p. 174.

[7] Downing, *op. cit.,* p. 226.

Multiple Counseling

Several writers use the terms "multiple" and "group" counseling interchangeably. Wright's efforts led to the conclusion that many similarities exist between multiple and group counseling.[8] Downing, however, differentiates between the two terms. He writes:

> Group counseling is somewhat narrower in its purpose and coverage of topics. The problems discussed and matters of concern are generally of the kind given consideration in a guidance service. The problems are personal but may not have the same depth, nor are they pursued with the same intensity, as those in multiple counseling.[9]

Group Counseling

Cohn, Combs, Gibian, and Sniffen have defined group counseling as "a dynamic, interpersonal process through which individuals in the normal range of adjustment work within a peer group and with a professionally trained counselor, exploring problems and feelings in an attempt to modify their attitudes so that they are better able to deal with developmental problems."[10]

Group counseling involves two or more people working by means of interpersonal relationships to discover possible solutions to problems. The relationships of the individuals within the group is a most important factor.[11] Group counseling helps the child to acquire social understanding, to develop habits of cooperation, and to better understand himself.

Group Counseling or Counseling in Groups?

The idea of counseling more than one student at a time is a relatively new concept for most school counselors. Considerable confusion and controversy concerning its nature and outcomes still persists. Some of the controversy centers around the issue of "group counseling" versus "counseling in groups." Proponents of the group counseling approach argue that the primary focus is upon members of the group, not upon the counselor. The counselor avoids assuming a central role. Each member of the group has the opportunity to act as

---

[8] E. Wayne Wright, "Multiple Counseling: Why? When? How?" *Personnel and Guidance Journal,* Vol. 37 (1959), pp. 551–59.

[9] Downing, *op. cit.,* p. 225.

[10] Benjamin Cohn, Charles F. Combs, Edward J. Gibian, and Mead A. Sniffen, "Group Counseling: An Orientation," *Personnel and Guidance Journal,* Vol. 42, No. 4 (December, 1963), pp. 355–58.

[11] Don Dinkmeyer (ed.), *Guidance and Counseling in the Elementary School* (New York: Holt, Rinehart & Winston, Inc., 1968), p. 271.

a helping person to other members. The counselor plays a facilitating role.

Those who hold an opposing view seem to suggest a "counseling in the group" method and maintain that relationships are between the counselor and each group member. They feel that the counselor assumes and maintains a central role in the group and that gains made by a group member result mainly from interaction with the counselor.[12]

Such arguments may relate more directly to individual interests and biases than to real problems or issues. The writer doubts whether the phenomenon of group counseling provides for such clear-cut relationships. The group counselor is a facilitator of group interaction, but he is also an active member of the group. At times he may assume the central role; at other times his role may be less direct, and movement and interaction may be between other members of the group. Each member has the freedom to relate to and to interact with any other member of the group. Thus, gains may be made as a result of relationships with any group member, including the counselor. In either case, the attitude and the philosophy of the counselor influence the nature of this process and greatly affect the outcomes of counseling.

The Nature of the Relationship

The counseling group constitutes a human relationship between and among members; it is an interaction between members and between the counselor and members. It is essentially a helping relationship. Dreikurs and Sonstegard state:

> An effective group counseling relationship is based on mutual respect. It does not mean that any member can do as he pleases. Firmness and kindness is necessary in all group counseling.[13]

The on going relationships between members of the group may be described as *dynamic* and *interpersonal*. It is through interaction that counselees learn the kind of cohesive relationships so necessary to the development of a problem-solving atmosphere. Most individuals are able to find personal meaning through the opportunity to live through personal experiences and to interact freely with others.[14]

---

[12] These points are discussed in some detail by John Gawrys and Bruce Brown in "Group Counseling: More Than a Catalyst," *The School Counselor,* Vol. 12, No. 4 (May, 1965), pp. 206–13.

[13] Rudolf Dreikurs and Manford Sonstegard, "Rationale of Group Counseling" in Don Dinkmeyer (ed.), *Guidance and Counseling in the Elementary School* (New York: Holt, Rinehart & Winston, Inc., 1968), p. 279.

[14] Cohn *et al., op. cit.*

The above suggests that benefits from group counseling depend in large measure upon meaningful interaction between group members and upon the strength of the group relationship.

Lifton believes that group counseling provides counselees the opportunity to explore their feelings and attitudes. At the same time, it requires group relationships that permit an individual the freedom to express his feelings freely and openly.[15]

Dinkmeyer writes that group counseling provides a means whereby the child's character is expressed through social interaction. Group counseling provides the child an opportunity for developing self-understanding. Members of a counseling group come to understand their own behavior by observing and identifying with the behavior of others. Commenting upon several additional advantages of group counseling, Dinkmeyer states:

> The process of group counseling enables members of a group to feel a genuine sense of belonging, regardless of any individual's shortcomings; indeed, the child often acquires a sense of belonging because of his shortcomings.
>
> Group counseling helps the child develop social interests. In the group situation he can show his concern for others and learn the give and take of life.[16]

Several of the above points are illustrated by the following segment of a group counseling session with fourth- and fifth-grade boys. Counselees in this group were selected because of their common problem of getting along with peers.

WADE: Mr. _________ is going to let me have the new balls and bat today. And I'm going to get my own team.

CARL: He gave them all to the big kids. . . . They won't even let us play. I'm gonna bring my own. My brother said, he said uh . . .

WADE: Aw, your brother, you're always telling about your brother. Next time he rides through our backyard, pow!

CHANDOIS: Arthur won't be here today, Mr. _________.

COUNSELOR: Oh. Is he in school?

CHANDOIS: Uh, his mother said he was sick.

WADE: Yeah, he's sick.

COUNSELOR: I see. [Silence]

COUNSELOR: Well, how are things going on the playground this week?

WADE: I'm going to choose up. Mr. _________ told me . . .

---

[15] Lifton, *op. cit.*

[16] Don Dinkmeyer, "Group Counseling," in Don Dinkmeyer (ed.), *Guidance and Counseling in the Elementary School* (New York: Holt, Rinehart & Winston, Inc., 1968), p. 272.

CARL: [Interrupting] They chase us off. One boy, his name is Jerry I think, he hit me with a mud ball. I'm going to get him back too, after school. They have all the balls and gloves and everything. They run down before lunch and get them all.

WADE: We maybe can go to the other field. Mr. __________ said he would see about it.

CARL: He ain't even here. He goes to the bowling alley at lunch every day. He gives Mrs. __________ and Mr. __________'s room all the balls and stuff.

COUNSELOR: You feel that your room should have some of the playground material.

CARL: Yeah. We're all supposed to play with it. But they won't choose none of us. They just laugh.

WADE: [Walking to window] See that yellow house and that big building?

COUNSELOR: Over there? Yes.

WADE: Well, we're going to play over there—and if they come over there, pow.

COUNSELOR: You're going to have your own lot.

WADE: Yeah, and they better not bother us either.

COUNSELOR: I see. Randy, have you played out there this week?

RANDY: No.

COUNSELOR: You didn't want to.

RANDY: Huh uh.

WADE: He stays inside and helps Miss __________.

RANDY: I don't either. I . . . [Silence]

COUNSELOR: Let's . . .

WADE: [Interrupts] He feeds the fish and waters the plants, and he gets Miss __________ cokes. [Laughs]

COUNSELOR: Let's see if we can talk some more about the playground at noon, O.K.?

CHANDOIS: Last time you said we could learn about us.

COUNSELOR: O.K. let's talk about us, and the use of the playground. Uh, what do you think about that?

The above is from the third of several sessions which the elementary school counselor conducted with this group. These sessions appeared to help the counselees develop some insight into their problems and feelings. Classroom teachers reported noticeable progress in three of the five counselees. Thus, it appears that group counseling did affect some positive changes.

THE GROUP COUNSELOR

Growth-producing group counseling requires interpersonal ties and relationships that are conducive to the personalization of the process and to the emergence of a genuine and cooperative self. The creation of an atmosphere in which growth can take place is largely dependent upon the counselor's skill in communication, his attitudes, his genuineness, and his understanding of group formations.

The group counselor must have not only good command of the techniques of counseling individuals, but he should also possess the techniques that are particularly applicable to group work. Techniques such as role playing, painting, drawing, and the use of puppets are sometimes effective with children. The group counselor is often called upon to use a wide range of techniques running the full gamut of the directive-nondirective continuum. He must be flexible enough to make adaptations and to play several roles in the group situation.[17]

Ohlsen, in a discussion of group counseling methods for children, states that young children require more structure and more carefully defined limits. He emphasizes that children in group counseling must understand how group counseling differs from classroom activity. Ohlsen also believes that group counseling with children requires more active participation on the part of the counselor than does work with an adolescent group.[18]

It goes without saying that the counselor must have a clear understanding of children, their developmental characteristics, and the influence of interpersonal relationships upon behavior. Again, it should be emphasized that the counselor must understand the somewhat dependent nature of elementary school children. Not only do they lack the sophistication and skill necessary to handle many of life's problems, but they often cannot make decisions without the approval of adults. Thus, it is often necessary to assist teachers and parents in understanding the purposes of group counseling.

The work of Cohn and his associates have pointed up some additional considerations for the group counselor. They write:

> The counselor must be a secure and accepting person. He must be able to accept the individuals in the group and to convey this feeling to them at all times, even when they question his motives. He must be secure enough to accept behavior aimed at testing his reactions to hostility and aggression directed toward him personally. At the same time he must be highly sensitive to the underlying feelings of the students.[19]

---

17 Cohn *et al., op. cit.,* p. 357.
18 Ohlsen, *op. cit.,* p. 290.
19 Cohn *et al., op. cit.,* pp. 357–58.

Group Counselees

Selection

There are certain basic principles which should govern the formation of a counseling group. First, since we are concerned here with counseling in schools, all children selected should be within the normal range. By normal, we mean that they are able to attend, participate in, and profit from regular school activities. It is preferable to select children who have some common concern or problem and who are willing to work toward a solution of that problem. For example, a group of underachievers may be formed on the basis of teacher recommendations. One elementary school counselor formed six counseling groups of children identified as isolates through teacher use of sociometrics. Other groups can be formed for children who have difficulties in peer relationships, or who have behavior problems.

Before selecting a child for a group, the counselor should interview the child individually so that the pupil understands what is expected of him and what he can expect from group counseling. Participation in the group must be voluntary.

At the elementary level it is generally preferable to segregate boys and girls for counseling purposes. Ohlsen favors mixed groups, but concedes that it may be wise to separate boys and girls at the elementary level.[20] Combs *et al.*, point out that the composition of the group will depend upon the maturity of its members.[21] At the elementary level, girls are usually more mature than boys, more able to verbalize, and more ready to discuss certain types of problems.

Group Size

The optimal size of a counseling group in the elementary school will depend upon such factors as the problem to be worked on, the maturity of the counselees, and the preference of the counselor. Groups of six to eight children are generally recommended. Mayer and Baker feel that the optimal group size at the elementary level is five or six. They suggest that with younger or immature children group sizes of less than five or six may be more appropriate.[22]

Children in the elementary grades are somewhat less capable of

[20] Ohlsen, *op. cit.*, p. 291.

[21] Charles F. Combs *et al.*, "Group Counseling: Applying the Technique," *The School Counselor,* Vol. 11, No. 1 (October, 1963), pp. 11–13.

[22] G. Roy Mayer, and Paul Baker, "Group Counseling with Elementary School Children: A Look at Group Size," *Elementary School Guidance and Counseling,* Vol. 1, No. 2 (March, 1967), pp. 140–43.

deferring their actions and reactions than older children. The elementary school child is neither as verbal nor as group-oriented as adolescents. Therefore, a small group of six to eight counselees would seem to provide the child with a greater opportunity to interact with his peers and to gain social experience than would a larger group.[23]

Advantages of Group Counseling

Several advantages are inherent in the group counseling process. The counseling group provides the child an opportunity to experiment in his own way with reality situations without fear of external action. For some children the counseling group may be the only setting in the school where the child can be accepted for what he is and have a genuine feeling of belonging. This is a unique experience within itself.[24] The group provides an opportunity for individuals to grow in self-confidence, to improve social skills, and to develop ways of reducing tensions.[25]

Peters, Shertzer, and Van Hoose make the point that certain needs of children can be met within the group. They write that the group can serve the following functions: (1) alerting the child to the rights of others, (2) showing that others have similar concerns, and (3) providing the child the opportunity to work out his identity in the group. The above authors observe that children acquire these needs in the following order.

1. The need to develop mutuality. This includes the needs for acceptance, the need to love, and the need to be loved.

2. The need to come to terms with authority. This function of the group is related to the control of behavior. In family situations the child accepts authority because there are stronger personal ties with an emotional quality; but in the peer group, which represents an optional experience, he learns to accept authority on a different and important basis.

3. The need to reevaluate. If adolescence is considered as a time when an individual shifts from the childhood world of fantasy to the adult world of realism, there is recognized a security which the peer group offers in helping to make this shift more gradual.

4. The need to relate oneself to a larger whole. As a part of social orientation the healthy personality comes to see himself as

---

23 *Ibid.*

24 Cohn *et al.*, *op. cit.*, p. 396.

25 Jane Warters, *Group Guidance* (New York: McGraw-Hill Book Co., 1960).

a part of a larger social entity. In a word, he learns the lesson of magnanimity.[26]

The objectives of group counseling are similar to those of individual counseling, that is, to aid the individual in developing a greater understanding of the self. In one sense, group counseling may be viewed as the stimulus or starting point for individual counseling but never as a substitute, for the personal one-to-one contact between a counselor and counselee. As Blocher points out, very few people advocate group counseling as a substitute for individual counseling. There is no evidence that group counseling conserves time or resources. Instead, group counseling is viewed as a positive approach for its own sake and can be effectively coordinated with individual counseling.[27]

Boy, Isaksen, and Pine believe that a basic value of group counseling lies in the opportunity it affords the counselor to establish contact with individuals who need a different kind of help from that found in individual counseling. Some students may find it easier to relate to a group of their peers in the presence of a counselor than to establish a one-to-one relationship with the counselor. There is often some supportive value to a counselee when he realizes that he is not alone in his feelings.[28]

How effective is group counseling as a method of producing positive changes in counselees? Research related to this question, particularly as it concerns children in the elementary school, is quite limited. However, a few recent reports of the outcomes of group counseling are most encouraging and are appropriate to our discussion here.

Lodato, Sokoloff, and Schwartz, conducted group counseling with slow-learning junior high school students in an effort to improve learning, their attitudes toward school, their peers, their teachers, and themselves. They reported positive changes in attitudes toward learning, toward teachers, and toward authority figures in most students. Students in their groups also showed positive changes in their self-concept for many students.[29]

Cohn and Sniffen have described their group counseling efforts

---

[26] Herman J. Peters, Bruce Shertzer, and William H. Van Hoose, *Guidance in Elementary Schools* (Chicago: Rand McNally & Co., 1965), pp. 169–70.

[27] Donald H. Blocher, *Developmental Counseling* (New York: The Ronald Press Co., 1966), p. 170.

[28] Angelo V. Boy, Henry L. Isaksen, and Gerald J. Pine, "Multiple Counseling: A Catalyst for Individual Counseling," *The School Counselor* Vol. 11, No. 1 (October, 1963).

[29] Francis J. Lodato, Martin A. Sokoloff, and Lester J. Schwartz, "Group Counseling as a Method of Modifying Attitudes in Slow Learners," *The School Counselor,* Vol. 12, No. 1 (October, 1964), pp. 27–29.

with eighth-grade boys who were underachieving and demonstrating negative behaviors. They report that group counseling helped students to develop a better understanding of themselves, to become more sensitive to the feelings of others, and to develop more positive attitudes toward school.[30]

An experimental study of group counseling at the elementary level was described by Kranzler, Mayer, Dyer, and Munger. They compared change in sociometric status of fourth grade pupils receiving counseling with those receiving only teacher guidance. They report some behavioral modifications with both groups, but suggest that their results seem to favor counseled students.

Group counseling with fourth-, fifth-, and sixth-grade boys was used by Kokovich. His counselees included students with behavior problems and those who were viewed by the teacher as most in need of counseling. Group counseling with these students appeared to produce more acceptable behavior, greater self-understanding, and more acceptance of teachers. Teachers also appeared to develop a better understanding of the students.[31]

Limitations of Group Counseling

While group counseling is viewed by the author as a method that can be used effectively by many elementary school counselors, it has some limitations that should be noted. One of the most serious of these is that not all counselors are qualified to do group counseling. Too often counselor preparation programs make no provision for giving the counselor course work or practicum experiences in working with groups. In spite of these conditions, the author has observed that many elementary school counselors appear to be attempting to solve the time and counselor-pupil ratio dilemma through group counseling. It is not argued here that group counseling requires *more* skill than individual counseling, rather that it requires some unique skills and attitudes that are not necessarily acquired as a consequence of experience in counseling individuals.

A second limitation or more appropriately a problem in group counseling with children relates to the problem of defining and clarifying the objectives of group counseling. Gains made by children in any endeavor are often dependent upon how adults who are involved with the child perceive the activity. Thus it becomes vitally important that teachers and parents understand the purposes and

---

30 Benjamin Cohn and Mead A. Sniffen, "A School Report on Group Counseling," *Personnel and Guidance Journal,* Vol. 43 (October, 1962), pp. 133–38.

31 Anthony Kokovich and Gerald Matthews, "An Elementary Principal Tries Group Guidance," *The School Counselor,* Vol. 12, No. 1 (October, 1964), pp. 6–10.

methods of group counseling in order to avoid misconceptions and misunderstandings.

Several additional limitations of group counseling are cited by Shertzer and Stone and by Shertzer and Peters:

> 1. Some students are unable to function in a group. Such students often need to experience a relationship with one individual before they are able to relate and interact with a group.[32]
>
> 2. In group counseling, the counselor's role and function becomes more diffused and more difficult. His contacts with individuals are diluted and his attempts at being one who is interested, accepting, and understanding, are more difficult to maintain.
>
> 3. The personal problems of group members may become secondary to the general problems of the group.
>
> 4. The presence of peers during a discussion of feelings and attitudes, while having a positive influence on some group members, may have negative influences on others. Some children are too fearful to reveal negative or unacceptable acts and feelings in the presence of their peers.[33]

Summary

Group counseling in the elementary school is a technique that can be used effectively with normal children. Just as with individual counseling, some modifications of the usual group techniques are necessary when working with children. For example, it may be necessary for the counselor to assume a more active role in the group than is necessary when counseling with an adolescent group. While group counseling is not a substitute for individual counseling, some children benefit greatly from interaction with a group of their peers.

Effective and healthy development is greatly dependent upon meaningful interaction with others. Group counseling can assist children in the process of learning to relate to others and it can serve to develop self-understanding as well as habits of group cooperation, planning, and problem solving. Because of the nature of the child's relationships with adults, i.e., teachers and parents, it is necessary that adults have some understanding of the purposes of group counseling in order to enhance the effectiveness of work done in the group.

---

[32] Shertzer and Stone, *op. cit.,* p. 177.

[33] Bruce Shertzer and Herman J. Peters, *Techniques for Individual Appraisal and Development* (New York: The Macmillan Co., 1965), p. 53.

Selected References

Boy, Angelo V., Isaksen, Henry L., and Pine, Gerald J. "Multiple Counseling: A Catalyst for Individual Counseling," *The School Counselor,* Vol. 11, No. 1 (October, 1963).

Cohn, Benjamin, Combs, Charles F., Gibian, Edward J., and Sniffen, Mead A. "Group Counseling: An Orientation," *Personnel and Guidance Journal* Vol. 42, No. 4 (December, 1963), pp. 355–58.

Cohn, Benjamin, and Sniffen, Mead A. "A School Report on Group Counseling," *Personnel and Guidance Journal,* Vol. 43 (October, 1962), pp. 133–38.

Combs, Charles F. "Group Counseling: Applying the Technique," *The School Counselor* Vol. 11, No. 1 (October, 1963).

Dinkmeyer, Don. "Group Counseling," *Guidance and Counseling in the Elementary School,* ed. Don Dinkmeyer, New York: Holt, Rinehart & Winston, Inc., 1968, p. 272.

Kranzler, Gerald D.; Mayer, George Roy; Dyer, Calvin O., and Munger, Paul F., "Counseling with Elementary School Children: An Experimental Study," *Personnel and Guidance Journal,* Vol. 44, No. 9 (May, 1966), pp. 944–49.

Mayer, G. Roy, and Baker, Paul. "Group Counseling with Elementary School Children: A Look at Group Size," *Elementary School Guidance and Counseling* Vol. 1, No. 2 (March, 1967), pp. 140–43.

Warters, Jane. *Group Guidance.* New York: McGraw-Hill Book Co., 1960.

PART IV

Consultation

CONSULTATION WITH TEACHERS AND PARENTS is an important function of the elementary school counselor. However, it is a secondary function and derives from the primary function of counseling.

The counselor as a consultant focuses upon the child or upon some matter or condition relating to the child. Consultation is a way of providing information, sharing information and ideas, clarifying problems, or developing a plan for assisting the pupil. It is a two-way process. That is, teachers or other adults may request counselor help or information on a matter involving the behavior or learning of a pupil, or the counselor may seek information from the teacher regarding a counselee.

It is recognized that the counselor may also serve as a consultant and resource person through staffing and in-service. In the latter example, several cautions should be noted. In-service relating to needs and behavior of pupils may be quite appropriate, but it may easily take on supervisory characteristics if the emphasis shifts to teachers and classroom practices.

While much consultation takes places with teachers and other school personnel, the counselor also consults frequently with parents. Because of the dependency role of elementary school children, it is often difficult to help a child without some attention to the child's home and parents. Thus, it may be necessary to affect changes in the parents' understanding of the situation and to attempt to change parent-child relationships.

Chapters 8 and 9 describe the consulting function and give some attention to the need for, and to methods of, consulting. The counselor is expected to have the understanding of children and the skill in developing the working relationships necessary for meaningful consultation.

Chapter 8

Consulting with Teachers and Other School Personnel

CONSULTATION BETWEEN COUNSELORS AND TEACHERS, and between counselors and other professionals is a cooperative effort aimed at providing for more adequate growth of pupils. Elementary school guidance is often viewed as a team effort, and it therefore follows that a frequent huddle to make plans and to discuss the best strategy is vitally important. By the very nature of his role in the school, the counselor is a key member of this team. He must often assume the responsibility for initiating conferences, either on a formal or informal basis.

The position taken here is that the counselor's work in helping teachers enhance the academic and social development of children can best be described as "consultative." The basic aim of consultation is to help a child. While the counselor may be perceived by some adults as a convenient source for psychological help on personal problems, the pitfalls inherent in personal counseling with one's professional colleagues are so obvious that no explanation is required in this presentation.

The counselor cannot develop an effective guidance program

without strong collaborative relationships with teachers and other members of the school staff. Thus, he should take the initiative in establishing these relationships and in developing free and open lines of communication between himself and other staff members. This requires that the counselor exhibit the same warmth and understanding that he has accepted as a necessary component of his work with students.

The guidance role of the teacher has been discussed by numerous authors. A point consistently emphasized in this text is that the teacher is a participating member of the guidance team. Hoyt adequately summarizes this view in the following statement:

> The classroom teacher must be viewed as the school counselor's chief professional ally in the attainment of guidance objectives. The teacher functions directly and actively as a guidance worker in identifying students in need of counseling, in student appraisal procedures, in increasing student self-understanding and understanding of environmental opportunities through classroom activities, and in follow-through of counseling carried out by the school counselor in terms of environmental manipulation within the classroom.[1]

If the teacher is to function effectively as a guidance worker, then she must understand her role in the program and she must be accepted by the counselor as a professional team member. The teacher has a right to expect frequent consultations with the counselor as she attempts to learn about the various social, physical, and intellectual factors in the personality of the child.

In his role as a consultant, the elementary school counselor is the chief catalytic agent for assisting teachers and other staff members in providing the environment that is most beneficial to the elementary school pupil. Kaczkowski has written:

> The consultative work of the counselor reflects a blending of his psychological orientation with the educational viewpoints of the school. It can be grouped into two main activities: *(a)* acting as the mediator between the child and his concerns and significant others (at times a child can only modify his behavior if significant persons in his life, i.e., teacher and parents, change their behavior toward him); and *(b)* helping teachers and other staff to examine the impact and consequences of instructional procedures on the child. The counselor helps the staff to evaluate the effective aspects of the instructional process. Since the school is a dominant force in the life of a child, the overall purpose of the

---

1 Kenneth B. Hoyt, "Guidance: A Constellation of Services," *Personnel and Guidance Journal,* Vol. 40 (1962), pp. 690–97.

school structures the consultative work of the counselor. The counselor, by counseling with children and consulting with teachers, helps to enhance the academic and social progress of the child.[2]

Brison describes counselor-teacher consultation as follows:

> In general, the counselor working in the elementary school would concentrate on contributing his psychological and counseling skills to the efforts of the teacher to help the child in the classroom. When combined, the skills of the well-trained teacher and the elementary counselor can more effectively develop the educational potential of children in the teacher's classroom. In addition, the bulk of the counselor's work would be with the large majority of children who do not have pathological emotional or behavior disorders and who are not mentally retarded.[3]

Thus, there appears to be considerable agreement that the elementary school counselor focuses on helping teachers further the development of children in their classrooms. It should be understood here that this function is carried out on three levels: (1) through consultation about individual children, (2) through staffing, and (3) serving as a consultant to the staff through in-service education. Most of the suggestions made throughout this chapter are pertinent to consultation on individual cases. Consultation through staffing and in-service are discussed in separate sections of this chapter.

Consulting Relationships

The conditions necessary for developing effective counseling relationships have already been discussed. While counseling and consultation are two different services, some of the same principles which apply to counseling are also applicable to consultation. In any consultation, the counselor must adhere to principles fundamental to all good human relationships, i.e., respect, honesty, trust, acceptance, and openness.

Several additional factors have a bearing upon the counselor's role and upon his effectiveness as a consultant to the school staff. Before any consultation takes place the counselor must be perceived as a person who is competent and willing to provide this service. This condition requires that the counselor be accepted as a staff member with specific skills which are necessary for problem solving through consultation. Second, staff members who consult with the counselor

---

[2] Henry Kaczkowski, "The Elementary School Counselor as a Consultant," *Elementary School Guidance and Counseling,* Vol. 1, No. 2 (March, 1967), pp. 103–04.

[3] D. W. Brison, "The Role of the Elementary Guidance Counselor," *National Elementary Principal,* Vol. 43, No. 5 (Spring, 1964), pp. 41–44.

must feel free to discuss any topic relating to the child and the school without fear of being penalized. As Van Hoose, Peters, and Leonard have stated:

> In conferring with teachers, counselors need to be especially cautious that they do not perceive themselves as accepting and understanding persons and the teacher as the authoritarian, restricting person.[4]

Purposes of Teacher-Counselor Consultation

One major purpose of consultation with teachers is to help the teacher gain more understanding of the situation and to acquire some skill in coping with problems in the school setting. The counselor also uses consultation as a method of involving teachers as team members in the guidance program. Kaczkowski believes that consultation can also be an effective method for helping teachers grow professionally. He writes that the task of the counselor is to provide the atmosphere whereby professional growth is possible by following the principles common to all human relationships.[5]

Ohlsen cogently points out that the counselor also consults with teachers when he needs help in understanding his counselees. Asking teachers to help him is often the best way for a counselor to develop a relationship which encourages teachers to seek his assistance, but it must not be done for that pupose. If it is done merely for the purpose of manipulating teachers into seeking his help, teachers will see it for what it is and resent it. Counselors do need teachers' help in understanding their counselees, but they should seek teacher assistance only when they feel a genuine need for it.[6]

Types of Teacher-Counselor Consultation

Shertzer and Pruett have described the range of counselor-teacher consultation. They state that the consulting role of the counselor includes:

> 1. Helping the teacher to understand the reason for the behavior of a particular pupil and suggesting classroom procedures designed to improve adjustment.
>
> 2. Helping the teacher to develop and use individual and group guidance techniques.

---

[4] William H. Van Hoose, Mildred Peters and George E. Leonard, *The Elementary School Counselors* (Detroit, Mich.: Wayne State University Press, 1967).

[5] Kaczkowski, *op. cit.*, p. 109.

[6] Merle M. Ohlsen, "A Rationale for the Elementary School Counselor," *Guidance Journal,* Vol. 5, No. 2 (Fall, 1966), pp. 57–58.

3. Assisting the teacher in the use of tests and other appraisal techniques.

4. Providing the teacher information about pupils which will help her in planning and conducting her classwork.

5. Other activities requiring frequent counselor-teacher consultation includes:

   a. Referrals.
   b. Orientation of new students.
   c. Parent conferences.
   d. Appraisal of characteristics and potentialities of students.
   e. Recording developmental progress of students.
   f. Public relations.[7]

In a description of their role as elementary school counselors, Frost and Frost list the following additional types of consultation with teachers:

A. Identification of children in need of special help and services.
B. Teaching about the world of work.
C. Special services available from the community.
D. The selection and use of guidance materials in the classroom.[8]

Consulting with Groups of Teachers

While consultation with teachers may be practiced most often through individual counselor-teacher contacts, some consultation also occurs in a group setting. Two of the most common types of consultation in groups take place through *(a)* in-service and *(b)* staffing, or multiple consultation. The purpose of the present discussion is to examine these two practices.

In-Service

Most in-service programs in which the counselor assists revolve around such topics as mental health, human development, and the needs of children. The counselor attempts to affect an ongoing program aimed at understanding the child as an individual and as a learner.

In this type of consultation, the counselor should avoid a purely classroom lecture type of approach. He should use information and illustrative data that teachers can use in their daily work with children. Teachers need to identify personally with the content and

---

[7] Bruce Shertzer and Rolla Pruett, *Guidance in the Elementary School,* Bulletin No. 247 (Indianapolis, Ind.: Indiana Department of Education, 1961), p. 23.

[8] Jack M. Frost and James A. Frost, *Elementary Guidance Handbook* (Grove City, Ohio: Southwestern City Schools, 1966), pp. 16–17.

ideas presented in in-service in order to apply this information to practices with children.

The counselor should provide specific suggestions on a number of mental health approaches to enhance the learning situation, especially those specifically designated guidance areas of educational and vocational development. He encourages teachers to work individually with children in classroom guidance activities.

In-service programs provide the counselor with a built-in opportunity for opening up communication with teachers and for describing to teachers how he can help them. He can convey his willingness to work with them through his actions and attitudes. If the counselor is truly committed and professionally competent, teachers will be quick to sense his desire to work cooperatively with them and their response will generally be positive. On the other hand, if teachers feel threatened by being "overconsulted" and if they feel that guidance activities are being forced upon them, any activities requiring their cooperation are likely to fail. Teachers need to feel that they are important participants in guidance from the start. Further, guidance must be related to the total educational program; it is not an end in itself. There must be a close relationship between guidance goals and the general goals of the school.

Staffing

In some cases multiple consultation with several professionals having contact with the child may be appropriate. This multiple consultation, or staffing, may involve teacher-counselor-principal, or teacher-social-worker-counselor, etc. The purpose of staffing is to exchange and clarify views, and to agree upon a plan of action. The counselor may also glean information useful in individual contacts with the child. It should be emphasized that such consultation takes place in a professional setting and in a professional manner. Confidentiality must be maintained. The counselee has the right to know when adults confer about him and he must be advised of plans developed as a result of consultation.

Consulting with Administrators

There should be little need to emphasize the fact that the counselor must have the support of the school administrator for whatever guidance activities he wishes to institute. The counselor should keep in mind that the administrator is not only responsible for the operation of the total school, but he is also responsible for the work of the school staff, including the counselor. His cooperation and support is vital to the success of the guidance program in that school. It is, therefore, crucial for the counselor to keep the principal well informed and to work closely with him. Stewart and Warnath emphasize this point:

> The principal is faced with repeated dilemmas arising out of conflicting demands from various parts of the school program. His responsibility, of course, must be to the total organization. He cannot approve activities on faith or because of theoretical considerations; therefore, the counselor should assume that the principal will require concrete and specific information about proposals related to guidance.[9]

The counselor, then, must confer frequently with his administrator on any project or activity related to guidance in that school. This continuing communication will help to increase the probability of the success of the program.

Harrison writes that frequent and professional consultation with the principal is necessary to the development of an effective program of guidance and counseling. She states:

> The counselor is a member of the principal's staff. However, as a specialist the counselor determines the specific *means* by which the desired guidance objectives are met.[10]

The elementary school counselors in one Ohio school system view consultation with administrators as one of their most important functions. In their *Handbook* they state:

> The counselors confer frequently with the administrator in order to:
> 1. Provide and interpret information about pupils which will aid the administrator in planning for the total program.
> 2. Keep him informed about guidance activities.
> 3. Help arrange for parent guidance activities such as orientation and special study groups.
> 4. Assist in developing sound pupil personnel policies within the school.
> 5. Help the administrator understand the reason for pupil behavior and to assist in developing procedures for the improvement of pupil adjustment on both an individual and a group basis.
> 6. Assist in planning in-service guidance meetings for the professional staff.

---

9 Lawrence H. Stewart and Charles F. Warnath, *The Counselor and Society* (Boston: Houghton Mifflin Co., 1965), p. 305.

10 Edna L. Harrison, "The Elementary School Counselor's Unique Position," *The School Counselor,* Vol. 11, No. 2 (December, 1963), p. 107.

Frost and Frost, authors of the above *Handbook,* believe that consultation with administrators should be viewed as a helping relationship. They write:

> The counselor should comprehend his consulting role as a helping relationship and understand that help can only be offered; it can never be forced on administrators. Caution should be exercised on the part of both counselor and administrator to prevent the assumption of the other's role. Each has a distinct role; the administrator should concern himself with instructional leadership; the primary concern of the counselor should be guidance functions.[11]

The principal will also need assurance that the counselor's activities are consistent with the primary goals of the school and that the total program will benefit from the work of the counselor. Further, the principal will want specific information on how the counselor perceives his role in the total program. While professional roles are never easily defined, the counselor can avoid problems and help define and clarify his functions through continuous and face-to-face communication with the principal.

Consulting with Other Pupil Personnel Workers

The elementary school counselor is one of the newest arrivals on the educational scene. He has joined with thousands of other pupil personnel workers in attempting "to insure that every child—the normal, the gifted and the handicapped—has an opportunity for a successful school experience."[12]

Eckerson and Smith have estimated that about 60,000 pupil personnel specialists are now serving pupils in the public schools. They include counselors, school social workers, attendance personnel, psychologists, speech and hearing therapists, and health specialists.[13]

All of these specialists consult with teachers, administrators, and with parents. Generally, they have achieved some status as professionals and have been accepted by teachers and other staff members as necessary to the educational enterprise. It is doubtful whether the elementary school counselor has yet achieved this status and acceptance. This condition is easily understood when one considers

[11] Frost and Frost, *op. cit.,* p. 18.

[12] Erasmus L. Hoch, "The Birth of a Commission," in U.S. Office of Education, *Scope of Pupil Personnel Services* (Washington, D.C.: U.S. Government Printing Office, 1966), p. 7.

[13] Louise O. Eckerson and Hyrum Smith, *The Scope of Pupil Personnel Services,* U.S. Office of Education (Washington, D.C.: U.S. Government Printing Office, 1966), p. 9.

that the practice of employing counselors for elementary school children is largely an event of the past two decades. This problem is further complicated by the fact that several programs have developed rather haphazardly and without sufficient attention to role definitions.

As more specialists are added at the elementary level, it is almost inevitable that some conflicts will develop over functions that are seen as common to both. Stewart and Warnath have indicated that a school may employ only one specialist at the beginning of an organized pupil personnel program. After a time his functions become broader than might be expected for his specialty. Later another specialist is employed, and the potential source of conflict is thus created. How the overlapping functions will be resolved depends, to a large extent, on the willingness and ability of the two specialists to place the welfare of students above their own personal feelings.[14]

As pupil personnel services are extended to all children in the elementary school, careful attention to distinct areas of service can help to minimize problems resulting from overlapping roles. At the present time, however, there is no universal agreement on the primary responsibility of the several specialists working in the schools. Conflict and confusion still exists particularly between elementary school counselors, social workers, and school psychologists. Different school systems place stronger emphasis upon some aspects of the program and provide greater rewards in the form of both salary and status to some pupil personnel positions. Supply and demand in the case of the psychologist, for example, have been factors which have contributed to his status and higher salary. Further, the school psychologist has gradually come to be regarded as the "expert" in dealing with children who present major problems in the school. His heavy and almost mystic reliance upon psychodiagnostics and his focus upon the seriously disturbed have marked him as the school "doctor" and have limited his effectiveness when we consider the total function of the school.

The work of the school social worker is in some ways similar to that of the school psychologist except that the social worker places more emphasis upon casework and less upon diagnosis. He is perceived by his school colleagues as problem oriented and he seems to prefer this image. He is generally so busy with his obligations to a small percentage of the school population that general consultative services in the realm of prevention and in the facilitation of healthy development of all children is virtually impossible.

---

[14] Stewart and Warnath, *op. cit.*, p. 307.

The above statements should not be interpreted as an attempt to minimize the importance of the work of other specialists. There is a great need for increased services for problem children. We need more specialists, not less. However, there is also a need for specialists who are skilled and dedicated to the total development of all children. Emphasis upon prevention and early identification through work with parents, teachers, and with the child himself can help to reduce the proportion of those who require extensive individual attention.

There is no shortage of work to be done in the pupil personnel area. Counselors, psychologists, and social workers have an obligation to boys and girls to work out their differences and then get on with the task. As indicated above, the development of effective working relationships between the several specialists requires that areas of service be carefully defined. Too, it is imperative that each specialist acquire an understanding of the professional competency of the others.

The defining of roles is only one step in the process of developing productive working relationships. If the guidance team in the elementary school is to function smoothly and if each specialist is to perform at his best, several rather specific procedures must be followed. The procedures discussed below may help to avoid confusion and thus make maximum use of the skills of the several specialists.

Referral Procedures

One of the most common sources of confusion results from the handling of referrals. When specialists describe their roles, they are, in effect, describing the types of cases they will handle. However, no matter how specific roles and functions are defined, problems often result unless each specialist has a clear understanding of how referrals are to be dealt with. Moreover, as Frost and Frost have pointed out, much confusion to teachers, parents, and administrators can result unless definite referral procedures are worked out.[15]

The elementary school counselor is generally a staff member of a particular school, whereas school psychologists and social workers may serve several schools. The latter are then used primarily as resource persons. The counselor must give some consideration to working with his administrator and to the teachers in his building as he attempts to develop procedures for referral. The specifics of the process can then be worked out with the other specialists. The practice of assigning the counselor some responsibility for screening

[15] Frost and Frost, *op. cit.*, p. 4.

referrals to other specialists seems quite logical. Since he is a resident pupil personnel specialist in one building he is in a good position to facilitate and coordinate referrals.[16]

Meetings of Specialists

If cooperative efforts are to be maximally effective, regular meetings of specialists working in the same schools are a necessity. Such meetings should be planned with the idea of each worker becoming acquainted with the other, both as an individual and as a professional. Through such meetings specialists can develop some understanding of the work being done by others and information and ideas can be shared and discussed. The complimentary roles of the several specialists can be accentuated through free and open face-to-face contact. Such professional contacts can also bring about a better understanding of school guidance.

The Role of the Counselor

As the resident pupil personnel specialist, the counselor should strive to provide the best possible services for the students in his building. He will find that other specialists bring a different orientation to the situation. However, he can make valuable use of these different ways of looking at the same problem. In fact, the differences in theoretical background and orientation provide the major strengths in the team approach.

In his role as a team member, the counselor accepts different ideas and different approaches and strives to synthesize these ideas in arriving at solutions to problems. He should set an example for openness and professionalism.

The counselor may encounter some status problems as we work with specialists who have a testing background or those who are oriented to abnormal psychology. This status problem may be coupled with the fear that counselors are usurping their functions and that eventually they will achieve greater acceptance and greater rewards. On the other hand some specialists may have legitimate concerns about the work of the counselor since many counselors are not in fact competent to function as true professionals.

The professional counselor should be able to overcome the above problems and in so doing develop the cooperation necessary for school-wide guidance programs. The extent to which he develops productive relationships with other specialists will depend upon his

---

[16] *Ibid.*, p. 4.

own attitudes and temperament and upon his professional understanding and know-how.

Summary

The major purpose of counselor-teacher consultation is to further the academic and emotional development of children. The effectiveness of the guidance program at the elementary level will be greatly influenced by the quality of the collaborative relationships between counselors and teachers.

The teacher often seeks consultative assistance in understanding the various social and intellectual factors that influence the behavior of the pupil in the classroom. The counselor also consults with the teacher when he needs her help in understanding a counselee.

Consultation with other school personnel may on occasion take on some of the characteristics of program development. It is imperative at this stage of development that all school personnel understand the role and the professional competency of the elementary school counselor. Further, agreements on cooperative working relationships require careful planning and discussion. Thus, the counselor will find it necessary to establish and maintain free and open contact with all school personnel.

Selected References

Brison, D. W. "The Role of the Elementary Guidance Counselor," *National Elementary Principal,* Vol. 43, No. 5 (Spring, 1964), pp. 41–44.

Frost, Jack M., and Frost, James A. *Elementary Guidance Handbook.* Grove City, Ohio: Southwestern City Schools, 1966.

Kaczkowski, Henry. "The Elementary School Counselor as a Consultant," *Elementary School Guidance and Counseling,* Vol. 1, No. 2 (March, 1967), pp. 103–04.

Ohlsen, Merle M. "A Rationale for the Elementary School Counselor," *Guidance Journal,* Vol. 5, No. 2 (Fall, 1966), pp. 57–58.

Shertzer, Bruce, and Pruett, Rolla. *Guidance in the Elementary School,* Bulletin No. 247. Indianapolis, Ind.: Indiana Department of Education, 1961.

Chapter 9

Consulting with Parents

Consulting with parents is one of the major functions of the elementary school counselor. Every counselor at the elementary level will find it necessary to have frequent contacts with parents both on an individual and group basis. In fact, the counselor has an obligation to provide consultative services to parents in order that all significant adults become involved in assisting children with school and personal adjustment problems.

Again, the term "consulting" is preferable to "counseling" in this context, since it is felt that the counselor *counsels* with children and *consults* or confers with adults. Further, the parent does not usually come to the counselor seeking psychological help for himself; he is seeking help for his child. The parent wants advice and information from a person whom he perceives as having some professional understanding and "know-how." Generally, the parent is not concerned with a clinical interpretation of the *why* of the child's problem. He is more often concerned about what can be done about it.

Secondly, the counselor does not seek a parent conference because of the parent's need for personal help. The counselor's interest in the parent hinges upon his concern for the child. The parent is the third party in the counseling activity. The focus is upon gaining and sharing information, and clarifying and analyzing reasons for behavior to the end that the school and the home can provide a more effective environment for the child. Working through and with a third party to better aid a child is often a complex and difficult task. The counselor is placed in the position of understanding the attitudes, anxieties, and feelings of two or more people in order to properly assist the child. Further, the counselor is dealing with the intertwined, complex, and emotionally laden parent-child relationship.

There are several sound techniques which the counselor can apply as he works with the parent. The particular technique which he employs in a given case is governed by a number of factors. The reason for the conference in the first place is one of these. Other factors such as the stability of the home, parental attitudes on child rearing, and the parents' own problems all need to be considered. The adroit counselor recognizes that each parent conference is unique. He makes adaptations as necessary while adhering to fundamental psychological principles.

The Parent's Role in Guidance

While parents cannot be expected to become child psychologists, they do have an obligation to understand the child's general level of performance in order that their expectations for him can be realistic. Further, parents have a role in helping a child meet some basic needs during both the preschool and the school years of their child.

Grams has written that the child receives his first guidance from his parents. He lists the following guidance roles for parents:

> 1. Meeting the child's basic need for love, acceptance, and security.
> 2. Helping the child learn to get along with others.
> 3. To stimulate continuously intellectual areas of special ability and talent.
> 4. To develop a scale of values for the child which will lend meaning to the educational experience.

If parents are to play an effective role in helping their children as individuals and as learners they must have some idea of the kind of ability the youngster possesses. Grams writes:

They should have some idea of how bright he is; where his strengths are, and where he is less capable . . . more important even than general ability appraisal, however, is an appreciation of a child's particular pattern of strengths and weaknesses. It is this variation which describes our uniqueness and which it is our function to develop.

Grams also believes that parents should be helped to understand the concept of "ongoing" readiness. While readiness is a term most frequently linked to kindergarten, the term readiness actually goes far beyond this special meaning. The idea of readiness relates to the fact that all learning builds upon previous learnings and its importance to the learning process is difficult to overestimate. The student who lacks the prerequisites for a particular course will probably have difficulty profiting as much from the experience as he would have had he been better prepared.[1]

The elementary school counselor can provide valuable assistance in helping parents develop understandings in the areas discussed above. He is the logical resource for information about the intellectual and affective status of the pupil.

Purposes of Parent-Counselor Conferences

Because of the nature of the dependency role of children, one way of helping the child is to help the parent. Since the behavior of the child is often causatively related to his interpersonal relationships with his parents, the counselor cannot fully understand the child unless he also understands the character of these relationships. For this reason, the elementary school counselor often needs to confer with parents while simultaneously counseling the child.

The major purposes of counselor-parent conferences are: (1) to provide parents with information that will enable them to better understand and help their child, (2) to interpret and clarify reasons for certain behaviors, (3) to secure information that will aid the counselor and the school to understand the child, (4) to identify unsound psychological practices and to help the parent reduce or eliminate such practices, (5) to help parents understand the child as a learner, and (6) to involve the parent in the school life of the child.

In all consultation the following basic tenets should be present: (1) The purpose of the conference should be clarified. (2) Understanding the roles and perceptions of each participant is a major goal.

[1] Armin Grams, *Facilitating Learning and Individual Development* (St. Paul, Minn.: Minnesota Department of Education, 1966), pp. 49–79.

(3) Consultation should be a learning experience for all persons involved. (4) Consultation is a collaborative effort at problem solving or prevention.[2]

Consultation is a helping process and should not be tainted with trouble for the child. It may be viewed as problem solving together. Van Hoose, Peters, and Leonard have emphasized this point:

> Meeting the parent with the attitude that we are mature adults exchanging ideas with each other for the purpose of helping a particular child make the maximum use of his capacities in a realistic manner lays the groundwork for healthy collaborative effort. Group meetings with parents and an understanding of normal development can provide common understandings that will help in later consultations.[3]

Dealing with Parental Attitudes

Parental attitudes play a most important role in shaping the attitudes and behavior of the child. Children who grow into successful adolescents and adults most generally come from homes where parental attitudes toward them were favorable and where a wholesome relationship existed between the parent and child. A good parent-child relationship is a necessary factor if the child is to be relatively free from anxiety, constructive, and happy.

By way of contrast, Gardner and associates have written that unsuccessful children are usually products of unfavorable parent-child relationships. The child who is deprived of attention and affection from his parents is hungry for affection. Furthermore, he is unwilling to please and to do things for others. This behavior is a form of compensation and an attempt to buy affection at any cost.[4]

Slater's illustration, Figure 1, shows how parental attitudes influence the personality development of the child. He believes that restrictive and demanding parents produce impulsive children. Warm, supportive parents produce spontaneous, gregarious children, and cold indifferent parents produce seclusive, socially withdrawn children.[5]

---

[2] William H. Van Hoose, Mildred Peters, and George E. Leonard, *The Elementary School Counselor* (Detroit: Wayne State University Press, 1966) , p. 62.

[3] *Ibid.*

[4] D. B. Gardner, G. R. Hawkes and L. G. Burchinal, "Noncontinuous Mothering in Infancy and Development in Later Childhood," *Child Development* Vol. 32 (1961), pp. 225–30.

[5] P. E. Slater, "Parental Behavior and Personality of the Child," *Journal of Genetic Psychology,* Vol. 101 (1962), pp. 53–68.

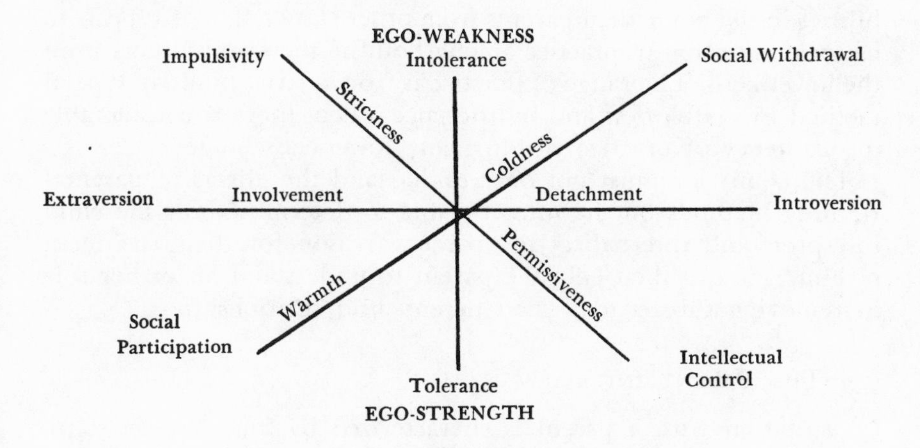

FIGURE 1

Relationship Between Perceived Parental Behavior and the Child's Personality

Counselors must acquire an understanding of parental attitudes and parent-child relationships if effective assistance is to be provided. The child cannot be understood just from within the context of the school. When the child in the home is understood, reasons for behavior become more visible and a positive plan of help can be developed.

Child-Rearing Practices

Several new attitudes toward child rearing have developed within this generation. This fact makes it difficult and even hazardous to generalize about variations in child-rearing methods and their influence upon the personality of the child. However, the counselor needs to have some knowledge of how certain child-rearing practices create problems for the child and of the variations of practice in our society.

Variations in child-rearing practices are found within the various social groups. Generally parents from rural areas are stricter and more authoritarian than urban parents. Fathers are on the whole firmer and stricter than mothers, and younger parents tend to be more democratic than older. Foreign-born parents are generally considered more authoritarian than native-born parents.

Social-class differences in child-rearing practices are marked. Middle-class parents begin training earlier, are more exacting in their expectations, and place more emphasis on individual achievement than lower-class parents. Middle-class parents tend to expect more from their children and require the child to assume more responsibilities in the home than parents from other classes. There appears to be great variation of practice among both mothers and fathers from the lower class. The range of practice is from a strict punitive type of method to inattention and indifference. Too, there is considerable inconsistency of practice within many lower-class homes.

The counselor must not only understand the effects of parental training methods but he must be able to determine how the child interprets and internalizes the parents' reason for their treatment of him. He can then help the parent to understand his or her role in removing threats to a good parent-child relationship.

THE PARENT INTERVIEW

Consultation with a parent is characterized by four distinct steps. First, the counselor must establish a proper working relationship with the parent. Second, he must try to understand the problem and the reasons for the parent's concern. Next, he must attempt to help the parent understand himself and his interaction with the child. The final step involves a plan of action designed to reduce or eliminate the problem.

Landy has made several suggestions that may be helpful to counselors in working with parents. He suggests that the counselor:

1. Indicate a willingness to listen and then really listen.
2. Do not accuse or blame either the parent or the school.
3. Say nothing if uncertain about how to respond or answer a question.
4. Avoid the twin temptations of sentimental sympathy and advice about situations on which they are not competent to give advice.
5. Avoid terms such as "lazy" in discussing the child's work or progress in school.
6. Try to discuss the problem in as nonthreatening and nonjudgmental way as possible.[6]

The interview with the parent should reveal the reason for the child's behavior. The initial interview, if properly conducted, establishes a constructive relationship between the counselor and the parent.[7]

During the first interview the counselor may find it helpful to the

[6] Edward Landy, "Working with Parents of Troubled Children," *NEA Journal,* Vol. XLIX (September, 1960), pp. 29–31.

[7] Manford Sonstegard, "A Rationale for Interviewing Parents," *The School Counselor,* Vol. 12, No. 2 (December, 1964), pp. 72–76.

parents to explain his role in the school. He should explain the reasons why he feels the conference is desirable and describe how the school and the parents can cooperate in aiding the child. He should communicate to the parents by words and actions that he is willing to help and that he is interested in their opinions and views.

Interviews with parents are guided by the same fundamental principles that apply in any interview situation. The interview should be governed by respect for the parent and respect for the child. An attitude of honesty, openness, and friendliness can break down barriers and help parents overcome much of the anxiety that they feel in conferring about their child.

Most parents know quite a lot about their child. However, many parents do not know whether behavior is normal or unusual. They are often not aware of the fact that each person passes through certain physical, mental, and emotional phases in the process of growing from infancy to adulthood. They are not informed about many of the normal developmental processes. Such understanding, acquired through consultation, can be most reassuring to parents and can help them anticipate and handle normal developmental problems with more confidence.

One of the most difficult problems which the counselor faces in working with parents results from the fact that some parents may overestimate his ability and skill in helping them solve a problem. Many parents come in expecting and wanting to be told. They want a quick, easy solution for a difficult problem. The experienced counselor will avoid giving pat answers and he will not feel threatened when he has no quick remedy. He will accept the fact that in some cases it is all right for him to say, "I don't know."

The counselor must also recognize that some parents have problems and anxieties not directly related to the child but which are nevertheless passed onto the child. Tensions arising from marital difficulties, economic problems, illness, death, and emotional instability are all factors that create problems for the child. When such problems are revealed during the interview the counselor has two responsibilities to the parent and the child. First, he can help the parent understand how such problems influence the behavior of the child and second, he can refer the parent to the appropriate person or agency for personal or family counseling.

In any consultation, confidentiality must be maintained. The fact that the counselee is a child in no way gives the counselor the right to violate or betray confidences. In fact, since the child is almost defenseless, the counselor has an even greater responsibility to make certain that he does not provide the adults with a weapon which can be used against the child. The counselor cannot risk making secret deals with the parents and he cannot align himself with either faction in a conflict.

Information Sought from the Interview

In a previous section it was noted that one purpose of consultation was to obtain further information about the child. The type of information needed is almost never spontaneously provided in any detail by the parent. The counselor will of necessity guide the parent in providing pertinent information so that he may gain more insight in certain critical areas. There are several standard forms well known to counselors which can be used for recording information from the parent interview. The form suggested in Figure 2 may be helpful when used merely as a frame-of-reference. Rigid adherence to the form, however, will result in a mechanical interview devoid of many of the nuances which a counselor can discover through a flexible approach to the interview.

FIGURE 2
PARENT INTERVIEW FORM*
CONFIDENTIAL

____
Counselor

____
Date

I. Name of Child____________________Sex______Age______
Date of Birth________________Place of Birth________________
Address ____
School____________________________ Grade__________

II. Father____________________________ Age__________
Place of Birth__________________________________
Address______________________ Phone____________
Education____________________ Occupation____________
Living in Home? Yes_______. No_______. ________________

III. Mother____________________________ Age__________
Place of Birth__________________________________
Address______________________ Phone____________
Education____________________ Occupation____________
Living in Home? Yes_______. No_______. ________________

IV. If child is not living with father or mother, explain:
____
____

V. Siblings:

Name	*Age*	*Relationship*	*Education*	*Occupation*

VI. Others living in home:

Name	*Age*	*Relationship*

VII. Does the child have any physical handicaps? ________. If yes, explain.

____

What corrective measures have been taken?

____

VIII. Has the child ever had psychological or psychiatric treatment? ______
If yes, give details.

____

IX. Social relationships of the child
- A. Ability to make friends
  1. With neighborhood children ______
  2. With classmates ______
  3. With adults ______
- B. Relationships with siblings: ______

X. Attitudes toward school
- A. Relationships with teachers ______
- B. School achievement ______
- C. Attendance ______
- D. How does he deal with adults? ______

XI. Impressions about the family:
- A. Stability ______
- B. Who is boss? ______
- C. Kind of punishment ______
- D. Kind of supervision ______
- E. Parents' attitudes about school ______
- F. Parents' plans for their children ______

XII. List any special talents or interests of the child ______

XIII. Check any of the following which apply to this child.

____School problems	____Reading problems
____Fearful	____Visual difficulty
____Selfish	____Hearing problems
____Jealous	____Speech defect
____Shy	____Restless
____Popular	____Stealing
____Aggressive	____Lying
____Disobedient	____Other ______

XIV. Counselor's comments:

____
____
____
____
____
____

* A similar form was developed by Elementary School Counselors in Southfield Public Schools, Southfield, Michigan.

Some Common Problems

While the type of problems which children present vary greatly according to the background of the child, the type of school they are in, and many other factors, certain problems are almost universal. Some of the more persistent developmental problems which the school counselor encounters in working with parents of elementary age children are discussed below. Pertinent suggestions which may facilitate work with both the child and the parent are given for each category. The counselor will also find the work of Gesell, Ilg, and Ames and others most helpful in understanding behaviorial norms for a particular age level. Reference should also be made to Chapter 3 which describes the nature and development of the child from 5 to 12.

Underachievement and Academic Difficulties

There is much evidence that underachievement results from conditions unrelated to the school. Furthermore, many children do not know why they work below their capacity even though they are constantly reminded by adults that they can improve. In spite of the fact that they get poor grades many underachievers actually like school even though their interest is likely to focus on nonacademic aspects.

Hurlock believes that underachievement is symptomatic of a variety of basic personal and social problems. She writes:

> Very rarely is underachievement the result of poor teaching or lack of educational opportunity; rather *the cause lies within the child himself.*[8]

Furthermore, the home and the school, per se, are not directly to blame, though they are indirectly at the basis of the trouble because

[8] Elizabeth B. Hurlock, *Child Development* (New York: McGraw-Hill Book Co., 1964), p. 629.

they promote emotional and personal problems which lead to difficulty.

The problems that lead to below average performance in school usually begin in the home and are often fostered by the school. The child from the strict home where pressures are placed on him to excel, and the child who is overprotected at home may both develop attitudes that are unfavorable to adequate success. Parents who are indifferent or who are negative toward education are likely to produce underachieving children. Family problems and homes broken by tragedy or divorce affect the child's outlook toward himself and interfere with achievement.

Certain school conditions intensify the child's unfavorable attitude toward school. The teacher's attitude and the classroom atmosphere are of major importance. Too, when the curriculum or instructional methods fail to take into account the interests and needs of the child, problems are likely to develop.

Many parents become extremely anxious about underachievement and transmit this concern and anxiety to the child. In most cases the more the parent pushes and prods the more hostile and antagonistic the child becomes. Some children, however, realizing that school success brings acceptance and status, accept the challenge and work up to capacity.

The serious thing about underachievement is that it is not a surface problem. As stated above, it is related to the basic personality structure of the individual. It may be difficult to correct without long-term treatment. For this reason the child's feelings and attitudes about himself, about school, and about those who press him to succeed, must be carefully considered.

One way in which the counselor assists the underachieving child, is through helping parents understand the complex nature of the problem and by advising them of the importance of their role in working with the child. For example, parents can be helped to understand that continuous demands on the child to provide evidence that he is working and "doing better" will often produce negative results. Secondly, the counselor offers parents some positive examples of aiding the underachiever. The counselor may, for example, give the parent suggestions on how they can show acceptance and affection for the child regardless of his school marks. Further, parents can be advised of ways to encourage without prodding, and to regard other accomplishments that are viewed as worthwhile. It may also be necessary to help the parent explore his own attitudes about his child's schoolwork as well as his aspirations for the child. Such exploration may help the parent in the development of more realistic expectations for the child.

Troublesome Behaviors

While most children frequently do things which parents consider "naughty" certain troublesome acts are almost universal. Some problems most commonly associated with the elementary school age child are discussed below:

1. Lying. Lying appears in the preschool years but it is more common during the years five to eight. In young children most untrue statements are not really meant to deceive but are mainly due to fantasy. Some false statements are primarily exaggerations, inaccuracies, and an imitation of statements made by adults. Pressures from adults, particularly teachers and parents, often encourage the child to lie. Too, some children lie to protect themselves against criticism or punishment.[9]

Older children tend to lie in order to protect themselves or to shift blame to others. By the late primary grades children realize that lying is wrong; however, they also realize that it may help them to avoid an unpleasant experience. Mussen and Distler point out that most lying in late childhood is due to fear of punishment, disapproval, or ridicule.[10]

2. Stealing. Most children learn at an early age that it is wrong to use the possessions of another without proper consent. However, in some subcultures stealing may be tolerated or even encouraged. The seriousness of stealing is therefore related to the values and ideals acquired as a result of early training. Generally, the act of stealing is interpreted as a more serious act as children become older.

3. Aggressiveness. One of the problems confronting most parents of school age children comes in the form of physical or verbal attacks on siblings and other children. Hurlock reports that such behavior is related directly to the child-rearing practices of the parents. If parents are unrealistic and inconsistent in their expectations for the child, problems usually result. Further, she notes that such behavior "is related to the immaturity of the child and is often provoked by the way in which discipline has been applied in the home."[11]

4. Truancy. Truancy becomes an increasingly common problem in the upper elementary grades. Many children who are truants come

---

[9] J. Macfarine, L. Allen and M. P. Honzik, "A Developmental Study of the Behavior Problems of Normal Children," University of California Press, 1954.

[10] Paul H. Mussen and L. Distler, "Child-Rearing Antecedents of Masculine Identification in Kindergarten Boys," *Child Development,* Vol. 31 (1960), pp. 89–100.

[11] Hurlock, *op. cit.,* p. 582.

from broken homes where older siblings and friends are also truants or delinquent. They are often doing poorly in school and frequently lack supervision and encouragement at home. Their study habits are usually poor. They exhibit such antisocial behavior as rudeness to the teacher, fighting, and stealing. On the other hand, some truants are from one-child homes or are children who are overprotected and pampered.

5. CHEATING. Many children cheat in school because of pressures from adults to get good grades. There is a tendency for boys to cheat more than girls and for children with low intelligence to cheat more than those who are bright. Children from poor homes tend to cheat more than those from better socioeconomic backgrounds. Children who do well in school have less reason to cheat than those whose work is poor.

The strong emphasis on grades and the pressure to succeed is particularly prevalent in many middle-class homes. Too, it is sometimes difficult to convince a child that "honesty is the best policy" when adults sometimes serve as such poor examples.

Difficulties in the Peer Group

Children are social beings, and during the elementary school years they become aware of their relationships to others and of others' reactions to them. While some subgroups appear during the primary grades, it is during the upper elementary years that peer group relationships take on a most significant meaning for the child.

The home and the school require a certain amount of group interaction and place pressure upon the child to get along with others. Being part of a group becomes most important and is most necessary to a major developmental task of learning to get along with others. Thus, interpersonal relationships during the elementary grades have several implications for future behavior and for success in school and in adult life.

Difficulties sometimes arise in the case of children who differ significantly from their peers. The difference may be in such areas as dress, speech, race, intelligence, or physical appearance. Most children reflect the attitudes of their parents or their community in matters of selecting friends, and in accepting or rejecting others. Children who are members of minority groups or who are too poor to dress like the other children may be rejected by their peers because of family and community attitudes. Some children also have difficulty in peer relationships because the teachings in the home have instilled habits that are different from the peer group. Whatever the cause, the child who is too different may be ostracized and ridiculed. The result may be withdrawal, the development of negative attitudes, and severe personality difficulties.

General Suggestions on Consultation

Because most parents are interested in their child and in his education they are concerned about any problem that interferes with school and his adjustments to life. The handling of such problems requires understanding and patience on the part of the parent.

Anxious parents are constantly asking for specific things which they can do to aid the child. The counselor can help parents to understand causes and to take constructive steps toward alleviating the difficulty. The counselor can encourage parents to talk with the child and to help him talk out his feelings with them. When parents realize that the child is often reacting to tension and frustration they can begin to accept the child and his total range of feelings. Brammer and Shostrom have written that when parents can accept negative feelings, yet remain firm about required behavior, the child can adopt socially acceptable behaviors with fewer tensions.[12]

The parent can also be encouraged to examine his relationships with the child and his method of handling problems related to the child's behavior. Some parents unconsciously encourage antisocial behavior through poor practices and through a lack of understanding in coping with problems as they arise.

Consulting with Parents in Groups

The elementary school counselor is in a most advantageous position to meet and to work with parent groups. In fact, the alert elementary school counselor will create opportunities to meet with parents and will be conscious of the need to keep the public informed about the school and about the work of the counselor. Some of the approaches to meeting and consulting with parents in groups are through (1) orientation programs, (2) child study groups, (3) parent advisory committees, and (4) parent-teacher organizations.

Orientation Programs

The elementary school counselor may find it advantageous to arrange meetings designed to orient parents to the school. Typically, such meetings are arranged for parents of students entering kinder-

---

[12] Lawrence M. Brammer and Everett L. Shostrom, *Therapeutic Psychology* (Englewood Cliffs, N.J.: Prentice-Hall, Inc., 1960), p. 346.

garten or first grade, and for those new to the community. Quite often such meetings involve all school personnel, i.e., teachers, administrators, special teachers, and pupil personnel workers.

In addition to such topics as school policies, grading practices, and special activities, the role of the counselor should be explicitly explained. Such meetings provide the counselor with an excellent opportunity for establishing friendly relationships with parents and may pave the way for future counselor-parent contacts.

Child Study Groups

In several communities parents are interested in securing help in understanding normal child growth processes. They are interested in having the school counselor assist them in developing a series of programs that will help them to better understand their child during the crucial years of middle childhood.

One school system reports that work with parents through child study groups is a normal part of the elementary school counselors' responsibilities. Their program grew out of the recognition of the fact that many parents are finding it increasingly difficult to perform some of the functions of parenthood in a complex society. The format for four meetings of parents, counselors, school psychologists, and social workers was as follows:

Session One

1. Introductions.
2. Plan of the meetings.
3. The school program.
4. Pupil personnel services.
5. Questions and discussion.

Session Two

1. Helping children grow.
2. Needs of children and youth.
3. The problems of a complex society.
4. Typical behavior.
5. Questions and discussion.

Session Three

1. Family relationships.
2. Factors influencing behavior.
3. The role of the parent.
4. The role of the school.
5. Small group meetings for questions and discussion.

Session Four

1. Meeting the challenge.
2. Danger signals.
3. Where to go for help.
4. Summing up.[13]

Parent Advisory Committees

Some elementary schools have found parent advisory groups to be particularly helpful in maintaining communication between the home and the school. Such groups can also serve as an important force in helping the total community to understand the importance of guidance and counseling in the elementary school.

The elementary school counselor may find that a parent advisory committee can be particularly helpful in planning special programs or activities—i.e., career guidance field trips, or orientation programs for new students and parents. The parent advisory committee can represent a systematic approach to involving parents in the school and in the guidance of children. Hoyt has suggested that the elementary school counselor should make widespread appeals for parents to come to the school to confer about their children.[14] The advisory committee can function in this capacity and can add considerable support to the guidance program.

Parent-Teacher Organizations

Parent-teacher organizations exist in most elementary schools. Such groups, therefore, provide the counselor with a ready-made vehicle through which he can develop periodic contacts with parents.

The counselor's purpose in working with parent-teacher groups is to describe his services and to define areas in which the school and home can cooperate to better aid the child. Counselor contacts with such groups can also develop mutual understanding and confidence and can provide support for the counseling program. Child study groups, as described above, may often be organized and conducted by the parent-teacher organization.

Peters, Shertzer, and Van Hoose emphasize that there are numerous matters relating to the education of children which the counselor can profitably bring to the attention of organized parent groups. They state:

---

[13] Jack M. Frost and James A. Frost, *Elementary Guidance Handbook* (Grove City, Ohio: Southwestern City Schools, 1966).

[14] Kenneth B. Hoyt, "Some Thoughts on Elementary School Guidance," *Elementary School Guidance and Counseling,* Vol. 1, No. 2 (March, 1967), p. 96.

The counselor can interest parents in guidance by discussing with them topics which parents have already expressed concern over or by dealing with problems on which parents often seek help. The counselor can also alert parents to the fact that many individual problems of parents and their children can best be handled in a private conference.[15]

SUMMARY

The influence of parents and the atmosphere of the home upon the growth and learning of children is visibly clear to those who work with children. Learning begins at home and by the time the child enters school he has already developed attitudes, habits, and aspirations that greatly influence his performance in school. The influence of the home can be either negative or positive. The school, and especially the counselor, needs to understand the impact of the home if work with pupils is to be most effective.

Most parents are interested in helping their children in school and in all aspects of living. However, they may often require assistance in understanding their child and in learning how they can contribute to his development. Elementary school counselors can provide much of this assistance. Through both individual and group consultation he can help parents understand what the child is experiencing and what the school is attempting to accomplish. In the specific sense, the parents can be helped to understand some of the dynamics of development of their own child and their influence upon his development.

---

[15] Herman J. Peters, Bruce Shertzer, and William H. Van Hoose, *Guidance in Elementary Schools* (Chicago: Rand McNally & Co., 1965), p. 192.

Selected References

Frost, Jack M., and Frost, James A. *Elementary School Guidance Handbook.* Grove City, Ohio: Southwestern City School, 1966.

Gardner, D. B., Hawkes, G. R., and Burchinal, L. G. "Noncontinuous Mothering in Infancy and Development in Later Childhood," *Child Development,* Vol. 32 (1961), pp. 225–30.

Grams, Armin. *Facilitating Learning and Individual Development.* St. Paul, Minn.: Minnesota Department of Education, 1966.

Hurlock, Elizabeth B. *Child Development.* New York: McGraw-Hill Book Co., 1964.

Landy, Edward. "Working with parents of Troubled Children," *National Education Association Journal,* Vol. XLIX (September, 1960), pp. 29–31.

Mussen, Paul H., and Distler, L. "Child-Rearing Antecedents of Masculine Identification in Kindergarten Boys," *Child Development,* Vol. 31 (1960), pp. 89–100.

Sonstegard, Manford. "A Rationale for Interviewing Parents," *The School Counselor,* Vol. 12, No. 2 (December, 1964), pp. 72–76.

Van Hoose, William H., Peters, Mildred, and Leonard, George E. *The Elementary School Counselor.* Detroit: Wayne State University Press, 1966, p. 62.

PART V

Professional Developments

COUNSELING AT THE ELEMENTARY LEVEL is receiving wide recognition as an important service in the school's effort to give each pupil an optimal school experience. Elementary school counselors are now employed in many schools throughout the country and there are several indications that the growth of elementary school counseling will continue. While there has been some uneven and perhaps chaotic growth, there has also been considerable progress. For the most part, elementary school counselors are doing a creditable job in helping children in all aspects of learning and living in the school and the larger society.

There are several issues in elementary school counseling that require the attention of all members of the counseling profession. These issues are discussed in Chapters 10 and 11. These chapters will be useful if they increase understanding of the present situation and if they stimulate meaningful discussion among elementary school counselors, counselor educators, and others interested in the progress of this movement. Chapter 12 describes the present status of elementary school guidance and provides some data on matters pertaining to certification, state standards, and professional background of counselors presently working at the elementary level. No doubt this status will soon change. However, it is presented with the hope that it may have some current value as well as historical significance.

Chapter 10

Professional Trends and Developments

THE FIRST PEOPLE to enter and practice a new line of work usually come from other occupations. New occupations are not generally established by youth who are just starting out. This is done by mature individuals who see a need or a new opportunity. The first people to enter a new occupation become the apostles, full of enthusiasm, and ready to spread the light and share the knowledge of their new field.[1]

The pioneers in a new field may bring with them some knowledge from their previous occupation which they adapt or modify to fit their new line of work. They also borrow from other fields having some relationship to their own. As they gain experience and acquire more understanding of the new occupation they begin the process of developing a body of knowledge and a set of techniques which can be used to prepare others to enter the new field. As the occupation expands, an attempt is made to provide formal training for new entrants.

Over two thirds of the counselors now working in elementary schools are former elementary teachers. Others are from secondary

[1] E. C. Hughes, *Men and Their Work,* (New York: The Free Press, 1958), p. 158.

teaching, school psychology, and social work.[2] Presumably, most elementary school counselors have some formal preparation for their new job; however, since models for counselor preparation at the elementary level were new or nonexistent a decade ago, it is unlikely that the first elementary school counselors received much specialized training for their new role. In fact, those who were formally trained as counselors probably received their training in a program devised for counselors of secondary school pupils. Aubrey notes that even those elementary school counselors who formerly taught at the elementary level are often indoctrinated in secondary models and procedures. Under such conditions programs at the elementary level often closely resembled those at the secondary level.[3]

In other cases the role of the elementary school counselor has been perceived as patching up problems. The counselor's identity has been confused with that of school psychologists and social workers and thus the counselor has worked primarily with deviant pupils. Such practice has been defended on the basis of the short supply of other pupil personnel workers.[4]

The elementary school counselor has been faced with the difficult task of establishing his own identity in the school while at the same time proving his value and justifying his reason for existence. He has had few or no models and very often only minimal support and assistance from those who might generally be expected to provide at least colleague support. As Hill has pointed out, secondary school counselors have shown a serious indifference to counseling in the elementary school.[5] Some pupil personnel workers have blindly resisted elementary school counseling, viewing the counselor as a trespasser upon their private domain.

In spite of these hurdles there is evidence of a trend toward acceptance of the elementary school counselor as "a professional of significance" in many schools.[6] The dedication, enthusiasm, and leadership of elementary school counselors have been major factors in creating a general awareness of the need and value of elementary school counseling. The elementary school counselor is performing a unique service that can be differentiated from other services provided in the

---

2 William H. Van Hoose and Catherine M. Vafakas, "Status of Guidance and Counseling in the Elementary School," *Personnel and Guidance Journal,* Vol. 46, No. 6 (February, 1968).

3 Roger F. Aubrey, "The Legitimacy of Elementary School Counseling: Some Unresolved Issues and Conflicts, *Personnel and Guidance Journal,* Vol. 46 (December, 1967), p. 356.

4 Louise O. Eckerson, "Realities Confronting Elementary School Guidance," *Personnel and Guidance Journal,* Vol. 46 (December, 1967), pp. 350-54.

5 George E. Hill, "Agreements in Practice of Guidance in the Elementary Schools," *Elementary School Guidance and Counseling,* Vol. 1, No. 3 (June, 1967), p. 194.

school. This fact is gradually being recognized by other educators and by the general public. Several trends relating to the emergence of the elementary school counselor as a key person in the elementary school are discussed in the succeeding sections of this chapter.

Toward Professionalism

Counseling is generally referred to as a profession and we seem to assume that by calling ourselves professionals and describing our work as professional we will somehow become a profession. However, it takes more than verbal reiteration to make a profession.[7]

McCully has written that school counseling does not meet the characteristics of other established professions but added that counseling may be moving in the direction of becoming a profession. He described six "developmental tasks" that must be achieved if school counseling is to reach professional status.

1. The unique social service the school counselor performs must be identified in a manner which will differentiate it from the services properly provided by all other staffs in the school setting.
2. Standards for the selection and training of school counselors must be developed and such standards must be acceptable to the corporate group of qualified school counselors as well as to those professional schools offering counselor preparation of high quality.
3. In order to make selection and training standards functional it will be necessary to develop a means of accrediting those institutions which meet such standards on at least a minimum basis.
4. In order to assure the public and prospective employers that entering school counselors possess at least minimum competence to perform their tasks, certification must be based on more valid estimates of minimum competence.
5. Qualified practitioner school counselors, severally, and as a corporate group, must actively involve themselves in winning and maintaining sufficient autonomy to permit them to perform their unique service in a professional manner; they must severally assume responsibility for their individual judgments and action in the performance of their unique service, and as a corporate group assume responsibility for safeguarding the interests of the public they serve.
6. The corporate group of qualified school counselors must possess and enforce a code of ethics governing the professional conduct of its members.[8]

---

[6] *Ibid.*, p. 193.

[7] C. Harold McCully, "The School Counselor: Strategy for Professionalization," *Personnel and Guidance Journal,* Vol. 40 (1962), pp. 681–89.

[8] *Ibid.*

Since no public or private agency has the function of determining whether an occupation has achieved professional status, the answer to the question whether counseling is a profession is a matter of opinion. Several people contend that counseling is already a profession; others believe it is not and may never become one. Still others feel the question is irrelevant in the first place.

When the status of counseling is analyzed with respect to the above tasks, it appears that considerable movement toward professionalization has taken place since McCully stated his position in 1962. While counselors generally have not yet achieved all the above tasks, many have been at least partially accomplished. Support for this contention is seen in such matters as more agreement on role definition, greater participation in professional associations, and higher standards for professional preparation and certification.

As McCully,[9] Richardson,[10] and others have pointed out, a profession has its origin in a recognized social need. Since the need cannot be serviced adequately by existing personnel, certain individuals are selected and given the training necessary to service the social need.

This writer believes that elementary school counselors have responded admirably to the challenge of servicing the guidance needs of elementary school children. They are eager to attain the competency and the expertise necessary for rendering their services to all children. They are dedicated to guidance and counseling and identify closely with their colleagues and with the professional associations. There is no doubt that, at this stage of development, the elementary school counselor is generally better trained, more involved in matters relating to guidance and counseling, and more concerned about the status of guidance and counseling, than was the case with his secondary school counterpart at a similar stage in development. Many elementary school counselors are assuming the leadership for defining their roles and for gaining the autonomy necessary to function as a professional. The activities of elementary school counselors described in Appendix A are not isolated examples; they are illustrative of the professional manner in which many elementary school counselors approach their new job. In some states elementary school counselors have already become actively involved in such matters as the development of appropriate preparation programs, upgrading state standards for guidance and counsel-

---

9 *Ibid.*

10 H. D. Richardson, "Preparation for Counseling as a Profession," *Counselor Education and Supervision,* (Winter, 1968), pp. 124–31.

ing, and counselor certification. Much effort along these lines is still of major importance.

Professional Identity

One mark of a profession is that its practitioners identify with it and see themselves as permanent members of the profession rather than as temporarily associated with it.[11] The professional is generally a member of his professional association, he participates in it, and contributes to it. He turns to the professional association for support, for direction, and for certain types of advice and information.

While there is no research evidence on elementary school counselor membership in such groups as the American Personnel and Guidance Association (APGA) and the American School Counselor Association (ASCA), this writer's observations have led him to the conclusion that a relatively large percentage of elementary school counselors do belong to the above groups. In localities where elementary school counselors have formed their own state associations, as for example in Michigan, New York, and California, membership in these state groups often exceeds 90 percent.[12] The high percentage of elementary school counselors who attend state and national level guidance meetings is further evidence of close identification with professional associations.

The tendency for elementary school counselors in some localities to form associations separate from or as subgroups of APGA or ASCA affiliate associations raises several questions. Is elementary school counseling so different from counseling at other levels that its practitioners are unable to find a professional home in established associations? Will this partial separation eventually lead to disassociation from APGA and ASCA? Are elementary school counselors simply trying to dramatize their differences and gain more status for themselves? Have APGA and ASCA groups contributed to this situation through remaining indifferent to what is happening in elementary school counseling?

There are no readily available answers for many of the above questions, however, it is obvious that too much splintering off creates conflict, divides loyalties, and unleashes a series of problems that may be impossible to resolve. This writer believes that elementary school counselors belong in APGA and ASCA, and as noted above, it appears that many do in fact identify closely with those associations.

---

11 Buford Stefflre, "What Price Professionalization?" *Personnel and Guidance Journal,* Vol. 42 (1964), pp. 654–59.

12 Data obtained from Michigan Elementary School Counselors Association, Detroit, Michigan, 1968.

However, many elementary school counselors believe that they have some unique professional needs and concerns which are not entirely provided for by existing associations. While maintaining their identity with APGA and ASCA, they appear to desire some arrangement whereby some professional matters relating most directly to counseling at the elementary level can be dealt with. It may be that the recently established state organizations will serve this function. On the other hand, it may be necessary to establish procedures whereby elementary school counselors groups can affiliate with the parent association, either at the state or national level.

Preparation Programs

In 1961, Hill and Nitzschke surveyed 154 counselor education institutions to determine whether they had planned programs for the preparation of elementary school counselors. They reported that 30 percent of the masters' and 50 percent of the doctoral programs made no distinction between training for elementary and secondary levels. Less than "two out of five programs were described without any qualifications as to their common intent for both elementary and secondary persons."[13] A follow-up study conducted by Nitzschke reported that out of 575 institutions, only 9 percent offered a preparatory program in elementary school guidance different from the secondary level.[14]

This condition may have changed somewhat within the past few years. The expansion of Title V-B of the National Defense Education Act to provide for elementary school guidance institutes may have had the effect of stimulating the development of ongoing programs for preparing elementary school counselors.

Most counselors and counselor educators seem to agree that there is a common core of preparation which should be required for all counselors. However, it can be argued that some areas of study may be more appropriate to one level than to another. The skill and understanding needed by the elementary school counselor differs at several points from those required of his colleagues in the secondary school. It is, therefore, logical to suggest that there should be some differentiation in the preparation program. The major roles of the

---

[13] George E. Hill and Dale F. Nitzschke, "Preparation Programs in Elementary School Guidance," *Personnel and Guidance Journal,* Vol. 40, No. 2 (October, 1961), pp. 155–59.

[14] Dale F. Nitzschke, "Preparation Programs in Elementary School Guidance—A Status Study," *Personnel and Guidance Journal,* Vol. 43, No. 3 (April, 1965), pp. 751–56.

elementary school counselor have been described as counseling, consulting, and coordinating. In order to properly perform these junctions the counselor should possess skill and understanding in the following areas:

1. The psychology of human development, personality dynamics, sociology of education, and the learning process. Skill in interpreting and using research findings in child development and other behavioral sciences.

2. Guidance philosophy, principles, and practices; the guidance needs of children, and the relationship of guidance to the total educational program.

3. Vocational development theories, their application at the elementary level, knowledge of materials, and techniques for using these materials with children.

4. Theories and techniques of individual counseling with special attention to techniques of counseling with children.

5. The use of group procedures in guidance and counseling.

6. The pupil with special needs; i.e., the gifted, the slow learner, the disadvantaged, and the maladjusted.

7. Individual appraisal, including the use of tests and non-test techniques in appraising the developmental status of pupils.

8. Skill in interpreting information about pupils and about guidance to teachers, administrators, other pupil personnel workers, and the general public.

9. Techniques of consulting with teachers, parents, and other pupil personnel workers.

10. The teamwork function in guidance, i.e., working with other specialists in the school and the community.

11. Supervised experience in counseling with children and consulting with adults.

12. Organizing the guidance program in the elementary school.

13. Selecting and disseminating appropriate guidance information to teachers and pupils.

14. Skill in designing and conducting research relating to pupil needs and characteristics, and to the effectiveness of guidance.

The elementary school counselor preparation program at Wayne State University is designed to provide the above understandings and skills. This program includes the following courses at the masters' level.

Required

Introduction to Guidance
Child Psychology
Group Guidance
Case Problems (Individual Analysis)
Psychological Testing
Guidance in Elementary Schools
Exceptional Children
Educational and Occupational Information
The Counseling Process
Either: Counseling Practicum or Internship
Seminar and Research

Electives

Minimum of two courses from:
Educational Sociology, Evaluation and Research, Philosophy of Education, or Educational Administration
Minimum of two courses outside education, usually in Psychology, Sociology, Social Work, or Anthropology

The above program was created under the premise that there is a common core of work which all counselors need. The points at which preparation for elementary school counselors deviates is in such courses as child psychology, elementary school guidance, internship, and practicum. In the internship and practicum, elementary school counselors work with elementary school children. The internship is an unpaid experience and requires a minimum of two days per week for one quarter working in an elementary school with an elementary school counselor.

During their work in such courses as the counseling process and the seminar, elementary school counselors focus much of their attention upon guidance in the elementary school. The course in guidance in the elementary school attempts to develop understanding and skill in such areas as developmental needs of children, interpreting these understandings to teachers and parents, consulting with teachers and other adults, organizing the guidance program, and working as a team member.

The American School Counselor Association and the Association for Counselor Education and Supervision are jointly involved in preparing standards for the preparation of elementary school counselors. Their standards are found in Appendix B.

The Challenge

In this chapter we have emphasized that several recent developments relating to the emerging profession of elementary school counseling may have far-reaching consequences for counselors and for elementary school children. These trends and developments, if properly understood and managed, can help to place elementary school counseling in the mainstream of American education. On the other hand, if the signals are misread, if directions are not followed, and if certain cautions are not observed, then the hurdles and problems may become insurmountable.

Elementary school counseling has been generally well accepted throughout the nation, and only a few persons have been openly critical of the movement. It may well be that this movement has flourished because educators and the lay public now fully recognize the need for counseling services for elementary school children. It is also possible that many people recognize a need for some type of additional service and are willing to *try* elementary school counseling. In either case it may soon be necessary for the counseling profession to provide some assurance that the elementary school counselor does make a difference and that he provides a service that is necessary and unique. This is a major challenge for elementary counselors and counselor educators. The need for research on counseling effectiveness has already been discussed, however, it should be emphasized that lack of research is a major need in counseling and until this void is at least partially filled many people will continue to question the legitimacy of counseling at the elementary level.

The second challenge relates directly to the attitudes of elementary school counselors. As noted above, this writer has observed that most elementary school counselors exhibit such healthy attitudes as enthusiasm, dedication, and excitement about this new field. This excitement is shared by many people, including the writer. However, we must not permit the recognition which we are now enjoying to obscure some very real problems. There is need to be objective in our attitudes if we are to give close scrutiny to several remaining issues and problems. The tendency toward smugness because of undisputed acceptance and high visibility must be avoided. Such attitudes lead to alienation from teachers and other school personnel.

The necessity for elementary school counselors to become more actively involved in matters relating to counselors and counseling in the school represents the third challenge. First, in their own school, the elementary counselor must insist upon enough autonomy to function as a counselor. This does not mean that he ignores school policy and that he cannot be called in question for his activities. He is a *school* counselor, a school staff member and as such reports to the school administrator. But just as the teacher insists upon the autonomy necessary to instruct, the counselor must insist upon enough elbow room to counsel. Secondly, at the state level and in such matters as state standards and certification codes, elementary school counselors individually and as a corporate group must insist upon standards that are consistent with the best principles of providing professional services to boys and girls. Third, involvement in and identification with professional associations is a must for the elementary school counselor. At this critical stage of development when attitudes and positions about elementary school counseling are taking shape, it is vitally important that practitioners in this field make their views known.

Some major steps in establishing standards for the preparation of counselors for elementary schools have already been taken. Several universities have developed quality programs through which the knowledge and skill necessary to the elementary school counseling function can be acquired. However, as Hill has pointed out, there is a woeful inadequacy in this area. There are too few quality preparation programs and not enough counselors are being trained.[15]

Inadequate preparation programs and a shortage of qualified counselors too often leads to the employment of minimally trained personnel. This practice has plagued counseling at the secondary level for many years. The elementary school counseling movement cannot afford the same mistake. Thus, the challenge lies in summoning the courage to insist that those who counsel with children possess at least the minimum qualifications as recommended by APGA. Children at the elementary level are too immature and pliable to be exposed to misinformed individuals posing as counselors.

The tasks that lie ahead are neither simple nor easy. They will not be achieved in a short period of time. They can be achieved, however, through careful planning and attention to strategy, and through the cooperative efforts of counselors, counselor educators and others interested in the elementary school guidance movement.

Summary

The elementary school counselor is faced with the challenging and exciting task of laying the foundations for a new field. One of his major tasks at this stage of development is to demonstrate that his function is different from teachers, from administrators, and from other pupil personnel workers. While carving out an identity for himself, the counselor in the elementary school must not disassociate himself from other educators. He must involve himself in professional matters and in professional associations.

Several challenges lie ahead. The major challenge lies in being

---

[15] Hill, *op. cit.*, p. 194.

courageous enough to insist that elementary counselors be adequately prepared, even in the face of the shortage of personnel. The future of the elementary school guidance movement depends in large measure upon the competency of the persons selected to perform the counseling function in the elementary school.

Selected References

Aubrey, Roger F. "The Legitimacy of Elementary School Counseling: Some Unresolved Issues and Conflicts," *Personnel and Guidance Journal,* Vol. 46 (December, 1967), p. 356.

Hill, George E., and Nitzschke, Dale F. "Preparation Programs in Elementary School Guidance," *Personnel and Guidance Journal,* Vol. 40, No. 2 (October, 1961), pp. 155–59.

McCully, C. Harold. "The School Counselor: Strategy for Professionalization," *Personnel and Guidance Journal,* Vol. 40 (1962), pp. 681–89.

Nitzschke, Dale F. "Preparation Programs in Elementary School Guidance—A Status Study," *Personnel and Guidance Journal,* Vol. 43, No. 8 (April, 1965), pp. 751–56.

Richardson, H. D. "Preparation for Counseling as a Profession," *Counselor Education and Supervision,* Winter, 1968, pp. 124–31.

Stefflre, Buford. "What Price Professionalization?" *Personnel and Guidance Journal,* Vol. 42 (1964), pp. 654–59.

Van Hoose, William H., and Vafakas, Catherine M. "Status of Guidance and Counseling in the Elementary School," *Personnel and Guidance Journal,* Vol. 46 (February, 1968).

Chapter 11

Issues in Elementary School Counseling

THE EXPANSION OF COUNSELING SERVICES at the elementary level is a relatively new event in elementary education. Such services have been desperately needed, and for the most part, have been welcomed as an important arrival on the educational scene. Evidence of the recent upsurge of interest in elementary school counseling is seen in federal financial support, the publication of a journal in the field, and the increasing number of journal articles dealing with guidance and counseling at the elementary level. These events all seem to be clear signs of real progress, and indeed, there is little doubt that progress has been made within the past two decades.

Eckerson points out that the movement has had a grass roots origin and that it developed in each community to meet the special needs of its pupils.[1] Further, many persons from other disciplines, and from other pupil personnel services have been involved in determining the direction for elementary school counseling. Consequently, varying emphases and points of view have emerged. Thus, counseling at the elementary level faces several issues and problems which should concern all members of the counseling profession. This chapter will

---

[1] Louise O. Eckerson, "Elementary School Guidance: Developments and Trends," in George H. Moreau (ed.), *Guidance Awareness in Elementary Education* (Washington, D.C.: National Catholic Educational Association, 1967), p. 1.

discuss some of these issues in an attempt to clarify some problems now confronting elementary school counselors and counselor educators.

Lack of Theory and Research

Aubrey has raised the question of whether it is fair to criticize recent developments in elementary school guidance for lack of firm foundations in theory and research. He goes on to point out, however, that it has been primarily individuals outside the field who have given us the theoretical foundations necessary to get started.[2]

Research voids in elementary school guidance have been described by Cottingham. He points out that in spite of the numerous recent publications in the field of elementary school guidance, few have devoted much space to the theoretical bases for either the guidance function or the counseling process in the elementary school. He notes that only a few attempts have been made to delineate theories which are uniquely applicable to counseling with children. This situation is due to a number of factors, including a paucity of empirical research on the nature and value of guidance and counseling at any level.[3]

This latter point has also received some attention from Stefflre who writes that guidance exists in schools because many educators believe it is a worthwhile activity, and not because of research evidence of its value. He lists six areas in need of research:

> 1. Agreement upon the terms used in guidance. Presently there is considerable confusion about the meaning of such terms as counseling, casework, consultation, and others.
> 2. More attention should be given to studying the process of guidance activity rather than its ultimate ends.
> 3. There is a need to temper our reliance upon quantificated sciences alone for our knowledge.
> 4. Research in guidance needs to be pertinent—not just to satisfy our whims.
> 5. There is a greater need for more conceptualization in the guidance area.
> 6. Demonstration projects could be helpful in showing the value of specific types of guidance activities.[4]

---

[2] Roger F. Aubrey, "The Legitimacy of Elementary School Counseling: Some Unresolved Issues and Conflicts," *Personnel and Guidance Journal,* Vol. 46, No. 4 (December, 1967), pp. 355–59.

[3] Harold F. Cottingham, "Research Voids in Elementary School Guidance," *Elementary School Guidance and Counseling,* Vol. 1, No. 3 (June, 1967), pp. 218–31.

[4] Buford Stefflre, "Research in Guidance: Horizons for the Future," *Theory into Practice,* Vol. 2 (1963), pp. 44–50.

The total guidance movement in this country is relatively new and at the elementary level the arrival of counselors in the school is such a recent event that many of the research deficiencies noted above are not surprising. Obviously some solid rationale should precede the inauguration of any program. It does not follow, however, that the theoretical rationale must be developed exclusively by those in the field. Neither is it always practical nor sensible to wait for universal agreement on theoretical foundations. In fact, considerable work by educators in and outside of the counseling profession as well as the thinking of several behavioral scientists has provided some strong foundations for the counseling service in the elementary school. For example, Gowan, Coole, and McDonald, in an excellent article, have described the contributions of Piaget to the guidance movement.[5] The developmental needs of children in the elementary school have been fully documented. Too, it is widely recognized that many of these needs are not presently being met. The counseling service is viewed by many well-informed educators and psychologists as one approach to meeting these needs. While the specific application of counseling with elementary school children is still in need of much attention, pioneering efforts in the direction of building theoretical foundations for counseling at the elementary level have been made by Peters,[6] Dinkmeyer,[7] Hill,[8] Faust,[9] and others.

The above statements in no way suggest that research attention focusing upon several aspects of counseling in the elementary school is unnecessary. On the contrary, much effort should be devoted to researching such matters as (1) the unmet needs of elementary school children, and (2) counseling approaches which are appropriate to helping children meet these needs.

There are several encouraging developments that may help to close the research and theory gap. Hill points to the work of such groups as the Interprofessional Research Commission on Pupil Personnel Services (IRCOPS) in disseminating research information to schools and universities. State departments of education are conducting pilot programs in an effort to determine the best approaches to

---

[5] John C. Gowan, Doris Coole, and Peggy McDonald, "The Impact of Piaget on Guidance," *Elementary School Guidance and Counseling,* Vol. 1, No. 3 (June, 1967), pp. 208–17.

[6] Herman J. Peters, "Differential Factors between Elementary and Secondary School Counseling," *The School Counselor,* Vol. 7 (1959), pp. 3–11.

[7] Don Dinkmeyer, "Counseling Theory and Practice in the Elementary School," *Elementary School Guidance and Counseling,* Vol. 1, No. 3 (June, 1967), pp. 196–207.

[8] George Hill, "The Start of a Continuous Program Is Guidance in the Elementary Schools," *The Clearing House,* Vol. 38, No. 2 (October, 1963), pp. 111–16.

[9] Verne Faust, "The Counselor as a Consultant to Teachers," *Elementary School Guidance and Counseling,* Vol. 1, No. 2 (March, 1967), pp. 112–17.

guidance and counseling for elementary school children.[10] Currently, Cottingham, working with a grant from the U.S. Office of Education, is conducting research for a position paper on the theoretical basis for guidance in the elementary school.

There is an obvious need for elementary school counselors and counselor educators to design and carry out research projects related to various aspects of the counseling activity. In particular, research and theory regarding the counseling process with normal children in the school setting is a necessity. Since the development of a sound theory requires practice as well as research, the elementary school counselor and the counselor educator must assume major responsibilities for developing the counseling theory most appropriate to working with elementary school children.

Role Definition

The matter of role definition for the elementary school counselor has received considerable attention in the literature. This concern and discussion is probably a healthy condition and hopefully will be favorable to the counseling profession. This writer has noted with interest that many of those who are the most vocal in decrying the confusion in this area are former secondary school counselors, who after several decades, have not yet adequately defined their own role.

Throughout this volume it has been emphasized that many needs of children in the elementary grades are not being met—not by teachers, administrators, or other pupil personnel workers. Too, there are distinct differences between the functions of teaching, administration, testing, etc., and the counseling function. Thus, role definitions for elementary school counselors require some attention to the unmet needs of pupils as well as consideration of the unique functions of the counselor. Aubrey makes this point in the following statements:

> Role definition is not simply a problem of carving out an area now neglected or mismanaged by teachers and administrators. Rather the difficulty lies in defining the characteristics that differentiate the teaching and the guidance function.[11]

McDougall and Reitan studied principals' perceptions of the elementary school counselor. They report that the four counselor functions rated as being very important by most of the elementary school

---

[10] George E. Hill, "Agreements in Practice of Guidance in the Elementary Schools," *Elementary School Guidance and Counseling,* Vol. 1, No. 3 (June, 1967), pp. 188–95.

[11] Aubrey, *op. cit.,* p. 357.

principals were all concerned with student counseling and parent consultation.[12]

Meeks, in reporting upon the work of the ASCA committee on elementary school guidance, writes that administrative opinion and actual practice reveal counselor functions that are compatible with the committee's thinking on the role of the elementary school counselor. The four functions consistently rated as important are concerned with: (1) pupil counseling and parent consultation, (2) identification of individual differences, needs, and problems, (3) working relationships with teachers, and (4) interpretation of the guidance program to the staff and community.[13]

The perceptions of elementary school counselors regarding their functions ought to receive primary attention in any efforts to define roles. A recent study of the role and function of 38 elementary school counselors in Michigan revealed those counselors spend approximately 60 percent of their time in counseling with children.[14]

The research, writing, and practice to date is indicative of considerable agreement on a threefold function of the elementary school counselor, i.e., counseling with pupils, consulting with teachers and parents, and coordinating the guidance activity.

The issue regarding role definition per se may no longer be crucial since there is much evidence that substantial agreement exists on what *ought* to be the major functions of the elementary school counselor. Rather, the problem may well be *who* defines the *actual* role of the elementary school counselors. Traditionally at the secondary level the administrator has largely determined the role of the counselor. The literature abounds with conciliatory statements about how the administrator has the responsibility for the total school program, including counseling, etc. The result of this kind of thinking has been near chaos with many so-called counselors performing functions that have little or no relationship to their professional training or to the needs of the youth they are supposed to serve. What is being said here is that too many administrators, either through lack of understanding of counseling, or in an attempt to remedy all school problems through the counseling office, have in fact grossly distorted the counseling function. Kehas argues that principals should not have the authority to prescribe duties of the counselor. He suggests that

[12] William P. McDougall and Henry N. Reitan, "The Elementary Counselor as Perceived by Elementary Principals," *Personnel and Guidance Journal,* Vol, 42 No. 4 (December, 1963), pp. 348–54.

[13] Anna Meeks, "Dimensions of Elementary School Guidance," *Elementary School Guidance and Counseling,* Vol. 1, No. 3 (June, 1967), pp. 163–87.

[14] Lois Brooks, "Duties of Elementary School Counselors," Wayne State University, 1967, mimeograph.

counselors should be responsible to a director of guidance for those activities involving services to individuals and to the principal in matters involving institutional responsibilities.[15]

Landy notes that many administrators who recognize their limitations in certain subject matter areas, and who are quite willing to allow specialists in those areas to organize and manage their own programs, often assume an expertise in guidance which they do not possess.[16] Elementary school counselors may face some of the same problems in their attempts to work with administrators and teachers.[17]

A related problem concerns the acceptance by counselors of roles assigned to them by school authorities who may be more concerned with institutional problems than with students. For as long as counselors remain passive in this matter, administrators will remain active in assigning quasi-administrative and clerical tasks to counselors. Counselors have some definite responsibilities to students, to the counseling profession, and to themselves, to assume a more active role in describing, defining, and demonstrating the place and the value of counseling in the educational process. The elementary school counselor, being new on the scene, is not bound by tradition or the activities of predecessors. He, therefore, has considerable opportunity to define his own role in such a way that the objectives of counseling can be achieved. Some elementary school counselors have avoided conflict and misunderstanding by carefully planning and discussing their role in the school with principals and other pupil personnel workers. Such planning and agreement should precede the initiation of the program and should help to prevent problems from developing over such matters as overlapping roles and confusion over counseling functions and administrative functions. Counselor role definition then, should be a matter of concern for administrators, other pupil personnel workers, counselor educators, teachers, and most of all, for the elementary school counselor.

Overlapping Roles

Specialists from several fields have been working with children and teachers in elementary schools for over half a century. Psychologists, social workers, speech and hearing therapists, physicians, psychiatrists, and nurses have all been involved with education and with

---

[15] Chris D. Kehas, "Administrative Structure and Guidance Theory," *Counselor Education and Supervision,* Vol. 4 (Spring, 1965), pp. 147–48.

[16] Edward Landy, "Who Does What in the Guidance Program?" *The School Counselor,* Vol. 10 (March, 1963), p. 115.

[17] Aubrey, *op. cit.,* p. 358.

special services for children. All of the above groups arrived on the scene several years ahead of the elementary school counselor, and all lay some claim to such functions as counseling and consultation.

If each of the above professionals do in fact counsel with children and consult with teachers and parents, then it must be concluded that schools have had a great variety of such services, and further that much overlap existed even before the arrival of the elementary school counselor. Overlap is inevitable when several specialists, working with the same population, provide similar services. However, the fact that one verbalizes a function does not mean that he actually performs it.

The problem of overlap is most visible between the elementary school counselor, the school social worker (or visiting teacher), and the school psychologist (or diagnostician). An analysis of the extent of overlap between the functions of these three specialists requires some consideration of such matters as professional preparation, ascribed roles, and primary orientation of personnel from each of the three fields.

The *professional preparation* of elementary school counselors, school social workers, and school psychologists is markedly different. Kelley describes the master's degree program for social workers as consisting of three major areas: (1) social welfare policy and services, (2) human behavior and the social environment, and (3) methods of social work practice.[18] Graduate preparation for school psychologists generally emphasizes understanding in such areas as child development, personality theory, juvenile delinquency, abnormal psychology, and the use of tests in diagnosis.[19]

The accepted core of professional preparation for school counselors includes understandings in guidance theory and practice, human growth and development, personality dynamics, learning theory, measurement, counseling theory and supervised counseling practice, and vocational development theory. In addition to the above areas, counselors are also given graduate preparation in such areas as anthropology, sociology, economics, political science, and philosophy. Laboratory experiences in counseling with both individuals and groups are also considered necessary in counselor preparation.

Elementary school counselors, school social workers, and school

---

[18] Jerry L. Kelley, "Social Work Services," in U.S. Office of Education, *Scope of Pupil Personnel Services* (Washington, D.C.: U.S. Government Printing Office, 1966), p. 37.

[19] Frances A. Mullen, "Psychological Services," in U.S. Office of Education, *Scope of Pupil Personnel Services* (Washington, D.C.: U.S. Government Printing Office, 1966), p. 59.

psychologists have different jobs to do in the school. Their *ascribed roles* are different. Rioux writes that the counselor assists students on educational and vocational matters, the school social worker helps students with special social and emotional problems.[20] Kelley describes the four services of school social workers as casework, collaboration, coordination, and consultation.[21]

The role of the school psychologist appears to be changing somewhat, nevertheless he is still functioning primarily as a tester. While he may have both the inclination and the skill necessary to perform a broader role, the exigencies of most school situations require that he devote most of his time to testing and diagnostic work. In some schools, the school psychologist works solely with pupils in special education and in programs for the emotionally disturbed. Mullen writes that "today the clinical function remains the predominant reason for the employment of school psychologists." The most common referral to the school psychologist is the child being considered for placement in a special class.[22]

The *orientation* which a professional has toward his work, along with his notions about what the important tasks are, must also be considered in any attempt to differentiate roles of specialists. The school social worker and the school psychologist have traditionally involved themselves with problem pupils and many seem to prefer to be identified as the expert on deviant pupils. Their professional journals, professional associations, and much of their research and writing activity focuses upon their work with abnormal pupils.

The elementary school counselor is neither a caseworker nor a tester. He lacks the professional preparation necessary for such functions and he was not employed to work with problem pupils. By the same logic, the school social worker and school psychologist have little or no preparation in guidance and counseling and should not assume an understanding and expertise which they do not possess. While they claim to counsel with pupils and consult with adults, some legitimate questions can be raised about these claims. Aside from their lack of training in guidance and counseling, the average social worker or school psychologist does not have access to most children in the school. Consequently, they are not in a favorable position to establish the continuous contacts and relationships necessary for counseling with children. As noted above, their referrals are the

---

[20] J. William Rioux, "School Social Work in the United States," *School Life,* Vol. 46 (August, 1964), pp. 9–10.

[21] Jerry L. Kelley, "Children with Problems: What Does the School Social Worker Do?" *National Education Association Journal,* Vol. 51 (January, 1962), pp. 54–57.

[22] Mullen, *op. cit.,* p. 52.

problem pupils who most generally require adjustive or remedial assistance. Whether this assistance is counseling depends largely upon one's definition of counseling.

Consultation by school social workers and psychologists is concerned in the main with a small segment of the school population. Further, since these specialists are in the school for only a day or so each week, the conditions necessary for close and collaborative efforts between teachers and specialists are sometimes nonexistent.

Careful consideration of the above factors lead to the following conclusions:

1. The professional preparation, professional orientation, and ascribed roles of elementary school counselors, school social workers, and school psychologists are different. While each specialist may have a general background in human growth and development, social workers and psychologists focus upon the pupil with problems. The counselor's concern is with all pupils and his emphasis is upon all aspects of development—academic, emotional, and vocational.

2. School social workers and school psychologists work mainly with individual pupils referred by adults. Counselors work with both individuals and groups and not only with adult referrals, but with children who refer themselves.

3. The elementary school counselor is a member of a building team and a colleague of teachers. The school social worker and school psychologists are generally viewed by teachers and other school personnel as itinerant specialists, working out of a central office, and with no particular ties to any school or staff.

4. In addition to his role as a counselor the elementary school counselor is involved with several other important guidance activities and with the total school program. School psychologists and school social workers appear to have neither the background nor the inclination to perform these guidance functions.

5. Some school social workers and school psychologists have attempted to avoid identification with schools and a few have been apologetic about working in education. Counselors in both elementary and secondary schools have traditionally felt a close identification with the school and have viewed teachers as their colleagues equally involved in helping all children gain the maximum from their educational experiences.

Viewed in this perspective, the question of overlapping roles is not a major one. Each specialist has a separate and unique job to do and if he performs the task within his area of responsibility and capability he will be fully occupied. While there may be some gray areas, i.e., in consulting with teachers and parents, such questions can generally be resolved through team planning and cooperation.

Counseling versus Consultation

In the previous section it was noted that most elementary school counselors and counselor educators seem to agree that the major functions of the counselor in elementary schools consist of counseling, consultation, and coordination. Thus, no *major* issue presently exists on these three functions. The real issue develops over the degree of emphasis to be placed upon these complimentary functions. Nelson points out that the local situation may in actuality determine the balance between counseling and consultation.[23] If several other pupil personnel workers, who have traditionally consulted with teachers and parents, are available, then it may well be that the elementary counselor can devote most of his time to counseling with students.

A major point to consider here is that consultation ought to flow out of counseling. That is, in the school situation consultation has the primary objective of changing the adult-child relationship through developing more understanding of the child. Thus, child counseling should precede consultation with adults, since it may be difficult to consult without information gained through counseling. Consultation based upon general knowledge of children is not sufficient. There must be a good understanding of the individual child. Further, all children who see the counselor neither require nor desire conferences between the counselor and his teacher or parents. Counseling children then should receive major emphasis and consultation should be done for the purpose of enhancing counselors', teachers', and parents' work with individuals and groups of children. While recognizing the necessity and the value of consultation, it is the feeling of the writer that a counselor's direct personal involvement with children produces benefits that cannot be realized by indirect assistance through consultation.

Confusion in Terminology

An additional issue develops when an attempt is made to differentiate between the terms counseling and consultation. The literature dealing with the various roles of the elementary school counselor frequently contains such phrases as "counseling with teachers," "consulting with teachers," "family counseling," "parent education" and "group therapy." The term "counseling," when used to describe

---

23 Richard Nelson, "Issues and Dialogue," *Elementary School Guidance and Counseling,* Vol. 1, No. 2 (March, 1967), pp. 147–51.

the elementary school counselor's relationships with adults, is most troublesome since it seems to imply personal psychological help for the adult. Likewise, the terms "family counseling" and "group therapy" used in connection with the counselor's contacts with parents also raise several questions. The first of these is whether such functions as counseling with teachers, group therapy, and family counseling are to be performed by a counselor with an educational-vocational orientation and one graduate degree (hopefully) in guidance and counseling. To label the counselor a consultant to teachers and parents is one thing, but to describe this function in terms that strongly suggest personal psychological help for the adult is misleading. The anxiety and mistrust that other professionals develop when they read that the elementary school counselor is a counselor for teachers or a family counselor can lead to unnecessary misunderstanding.

Several studies have shown that elementary teachers do feel a need for consultative services as an aid to their work with children, but to the writer's knowledge, there is no evidence that teachers have expressed a need for personal counseling, at least not from a school counselor. The elementary school counselor will find it helpful to consult frequently with parents on matters pertaining to children but he has neither the time nor the training necessary to engage in family counseling.

The writer is aware of the fact that the above statements may lead to the conclusion that mountains are being made out of molehills. However, elementary school counseling is a new and challenging field and there is a great need to use terms that can be understood by other educators and the general public. There are major differences between counseling and consultation and these differences should be clearly spelled out in the literature.

Titles

The titles "counselor," "consultant," "guidance worker," "guidance specialist," and others are used to describe persons working in guidance and counseling at the elementary level. Hill notes that some school psychologists and school social workers are called counselors.[24] Smith and Eckerson apply the term "guidance specialists" to all pupil personnel workers in their survey "since these specialists are working in programs labeled elementary school guidance."[25] Some cynics may wonder whether the expansion of

[24] Hill, *op. cit.*, p. 193.

[25] Hyrum M. Smith and Louise O. Eckerson, *Guidance Services in Elementary Schools*, U.S. Office of Education (Washington, D.C.: U.S. Government Printing Office, 1966).

Title V, National Defense Education Act, or the passage of Title I, Elementary and Secondary Education Act, suddenly transformed several other pupil personnel workers into counselors.

The primary objective of placing guidance personnel in the elementary school is or ought to be to work with *all* children. His chief concern is with children in all aspects of development. While he may consult, coordinate, and evaluate, his primary function is counseling with children. He should be called a *counselor*.

Persons who are employed to work with *some* children, i.e., problem pupils, may not be prepared to counsel children and probably would not have been prepared in a counselor education program.[26] To call them counselors is confusing to children, teachers, and parents, and creates numerous problems relating to the emerging role of the elementary school counselor.

Counselor or Child Development Consultant?

Patterson[27] and Nelson[28] have recently called attention to the possibility that federal legislation may be enacted to provide for the preparation and support of child development consultants in the elementary schools. Patterson notes that the thinking in the U.S. Office of Education seems to be in the direction of providing child development consultants rather than counselors in elementary schools. He believes that the basis for this thinking is unsound.[29]

Nelson, quoting from the proposed bill, points out that the child development consultant would:

1. Assist elementary school personnel with the individual learning and behavior problems of elementary school children, as well as with the educational progress of such children;
2. Assist school personnel in the recognition of elementary school children who have or who are developing serious emotional, learning, or behavior problems, and in making effective school-related changes to help such children; and
3. Assist teachers, parents, and school staff to become knowledgeable about community and other resources for the use of such children and families requiring assistance in the solution of such problems of elementary school children [H.R. 11322, 89th Congress, pp. 20–21].

---

26 See C. H. Patterson, "Elementary School Counselor or Child Development Consultant?" *Personnel and Guidance Journal,* Vol. 46 (September, 1967), pp. 75–76. See also Richard P. Koeppe, "The Elementary School Counselor—What Is He?" *The School Counselor,* Vol. 12 (October, 1964), pp. 11–14.

27 Patterson, *op. cit.*

28 Nelson, *op. cit.*

29 Patterson, *op. cit.*

It should be noted that the proposed legislation provides for consultants to teachers, other school personnel, and parents. There is no mention of counseling with children. Therefore, if the child development consultant replaces the counselor, there probably will be no counseling in the elementary school. Patterson doubts whether many schools could or would provide both an elementary school counselor and a child development consultant. He states that the justification for a child development consultant is difficult if the schools have adequately prepared psychologists, social workers, and counselors.[30] It is also difficult to justify personnel who would be limited to working with primary grade children.

Nelson[31] notes that Hoyt voiced his objection to the concept of a child development consultant:

> . . . primarily on the basis of objecting to the addition of yet another specialist in the general area of pupil personnel services in the elementary school. It was, I think, the feeling of the council and it certainly was my feeling at that time that we have enough problems right now identifying proper roles and functions for the specialists which already exists—that is, the elementary school counselor, school psychologist, and the school social worker. I did not feel that we could be making a positive contribution by adding yet another specialist to this array before we had clearly defined roles and functions for each of these.

Legislation providing for the preparation and employment of child development consultants in elementary schools would bring about some changes in elementary school guidance. Such legislation may retard progress and add more confusion to the problem of overlapping roles of several specialists. However, it is felt that the counselor in the elementary school is on his way toward acceptance as a vital member of the educational team and it is unlikely that a child development consultant in the form being proposed would displace him.

Federal Financial Support

Financial support by the federal government has had the effect of rapidly accelerating the progress of elementary school guidance and counseling. The 1964 expansion of Title VB, National Defense Education Act, to provide for the preparation and employment of elementary school counselors, and the enactment of the Elementary and Secondary Education Act are generally viewed as most beneficial to

---

30 *Ibid.*
31 Nelson, *op. cit.*

elementary school guidance. If there are benefits in numbers alone, then the above legislation has been most worthwhile.

A report of a recent survey reveals that approximately 70 percent of all elementary school counselors employed are supported in part by federal funds. The largest number are employed by funds from Title I, Elementary and Secondary Education Act. Less than 25 percent are supported by state or local funds.[32]

Our purpose here is not to debate federal versus local or state responsibilities, and control. We have no quarrel with the idea of federal aid; in fact, it is our contention that guidance deserves more financial support from all levels of government. The questions that ought to be raised relate to the manner in which programs of preparation and support are funded by Washington and to the criteria used to judge the appropriateness and soundness of proposed programs. Members of the counseling profession should also concern themselves with what amounts to arbitary policy making by personnel whose motives, judgment, and qualifications are open to question. Two examples pertaining to funding of institutes illustrate the above point.

1. Refusal of the U.S. Office of Education to continue support for an elementary school guidance institute because the concept of the elementary school counselor as a consultant was not emphasized.
2. Support for an institute under Title VB for the training of social work aides. The general announcement categorized this institute as guidance.

In the matter of support to schools for the employment of elementary school counselors, the writer has observed that elementary school guidance suddenly becomes a must when some school systems smell federal money. In such an enlightened state of mind they often give little thought to planning or staffing the program until the long-anticipated telegram arrives from Washington. The disastrous results of such methods can have a most negative effect upon elementary school guidance.

Again, it is not implied here that legislation such as Title VB, National Defense Education Act, or Title I, Elementary and Secondary Education Act, is wrong. In fact, many excellent programs are now underway as a direct consequence of such assistance. On the

[32] William H. Van Hoose and Catherine M. Vafakas, "Status of Guidance and Counseling in the Elementary School," *Personnel and Guidance Journal,* Vol. 46 (February, 1968), pp. 536–39.

other hand, the no strings attached, no directions approach, particularly under Title I, Elementary and Secondary Education Act, has also led to numerous abuses. The fact is that many so-called elementary school guidance programs have been developed with federal moneys without regard for (1) needs of pupils, (2) objectives, and (3) without any system for evaluating guidance effectiveness. Many such programs are staffed by unqualified personnel. These are major problems for the counseling profession and to ignore them is to invite chaos.

Summary

This chapter has dealt with only a few of the many issues in elementary school counseling. While space does not permit discussion of additional matters, there are several other questions that should be considered. For example, when listing the functions of the counselor, we are now secure in our belief that these functions consist of counseling, consultation, and coordination. Can a troika proceed in one direction? Does consultation flow out of counseling or vice versa? Must the counselor always coordinate, or are there situations in which this function may be performed by some other professional? Are counselor education institutions really preparing counselors for elementary schools?

These are only a few of the many questions in this field. Counselors and counselor educators have some major responsibilities for answering these questions. The final answers, however, must merit much wider support. Thus, teachers, administrators, other professionals, and interested citizens must also be considered. How these questions are answered is of great importance to children and to society.

Selected References

Aubrey, Roger F. "The Legitimacy of Elementary School Counseling: Some Unresolved Issues and Conflicts," *Personnel and Guidance Journal,* Vol. 46, No. 4 (December, 1967), pp. 355–59.

Cottingham, Harold F. "Research Voids in Elementary School Guidance," *Elementary School Guidance and Counseling,* Vol. 1, No. 3 (June, 1967), pp. 218–31.

Gowan, John C., Coole, Doris, and McDonald, Peggy. "The Impact of Piaget on Guidance," *Elementary School Guidance and Counseling,* Vol. 1, No. 3 (June, 1967), pp. 208–17.

Hill, George E. "Agreements in Practice of Guidance in the Elementary Schools," *Elementary School Guidance and Counseling,* Vol. 1, No. 3 (June, 1967), pp. 188–95.

Kehas, Chris D. "Administrative Structure and Guidance Theory," *Counselor Education and Supervision,* Vol. 4 (Spring, 1965), pp. 147–48.

Kelley, Jerry L. "Social Work Services," (U.S. Office of Education, *Scope of Pupil Personnel Services.)* Washington, D.C.: U.S. Government Printing Office, 1966.

Kelley, Jerry L. "Children with Problems: What Does the School Social Worker Do?" *National Education Association Journal,* Vol. 51 (January, 1962).

McDougall, William P., and Reitan, Henry N. "The Elementary Counselor as Perceived by Elementary Principals," *Personnel and Guidance Journal,* Vol. 42, No. 4 (December, 1963), pp. 348–54.

Meeks, Anna. "Dimensions of Elementary School Guidance," *Elementary School Guidance and Counseling,* Vol. 1, No. 3 (June, 1967), pp. 163–87.

Mullen, Frances A. "Psychological Services." (U.S. Office of Education, *Scope of Pupil Personnel Services.)* Washington, D.C.: U.S. Government Printing Office, 1966.

Rioux, J. William. "School Social Work in the United States," *School Life,* Vol. 46 (August, 1964), pp. 9–10.

Smith, Hyrum M., and Eckerson, Louise O. *Guidance Services in Elementary Schools: A National Survey.* U.S. Office of Education. Washington, D.C.: U.S. Government Printing Office, 1966.

Stefflre, Buford. "Research in Guidance: Horizons for the Future," *Theory into Practice,* Vol. 2, 1963, pp. 44–50.

Van Hoose, William H., and Vafakas, Catherine M. "Status of Guidance and Counseling in the Elementary Schools," *Personnel and Guidance Journal,* Vol. 46 (February, 1968), pp. 536–39.

Chapter 12

Status of Elementary School Counseling

The expansion of guidance and counseling at the elementary level has been discussed by numerous writers. The professional periodicals contain reports of surveys and estimates which lead to the implication that counselors are now serving pupils in a large number of elementary schools. Other reports contain references to *guidance specialists* or *child development consultants* when describing the staffing of elementary guidance programs. Careful analysis of these reports often reveals that many of these elementary school pupil personnel workers are in actuality social workers and psychologists, not counselors.

This chapter deals specifically with *elementary school counselors.* Other pupil personnel workers such as psychologists, social workers, and/or child development consultants were excluded from the national survey which provided the material for much of this chapter.[1]

---

[1] Catherine M. Vafakas conducted the survey and prepared the initial report, "Status of Guidance and Counseling in the Elementary School." See also, William Van Hoose and Catherine M. Vafakas, "Status of Guidance and Counseling in the Elementary School," *Personnel and Guidance Journal,* Vol. 46 (February, 1968), pp. 536–39.

Number Of Counselors

Data from the above reports, based on a 1967 survey from all 50 states and the 4 American territories, reveals that 3,837 counselors were working in elementary schools in 48 states. Two states and the four territories reported that they had no elementary school counselors. Table 4 shows the breakdown of the number and percent of elementary school counselors by geographic region.

Although the highest percentage of elementary schools with counselors are in the Southwest, the North Atlantic region (New England and mideast) has the largest number of elementary counselors. Smith and Eckerson also found the North Atlantic region to have the greatest proportion of child development consultants.[2] The Rocky Mountain region employs the smallest number of elementary school counselors: however, the Plains area has the largest percentage of schools without the services of a counselor.

TABLE 4

Number and Percent of Elementary School Counselors by Geographic Region

	Elementary Counselors	
Region	*Number*	*Percent*
New England	484	13
Mideast	948	25
Southeast	708	18
Great Lakes	367	10
Plains	277	7
Southwest	439	11
Rocky Mountains	86	2
Far West	528	14
Total	3,837	100

Previous Profession

The majority of elementary school counselors have held prior positions as elementary teachers. In fact, 67 percent of those in the Van Hoose and Vafakas study are former elementary teachers, while 7 percent were from the ranks of secondary teaching. Less than 3 percent were former secondary counselors. A small percentage are former social workers, psychologists, and special education teachers.[3] This finding is consistent with reports of Norris who found that the highest percentage of personnel graduating from counselor training programs were former teachers.[4] In the study conducted by Smith

---

2 Hyrum Smith and Louise O. Eckerson, *Guidance Services in Elementary Schools: A National Survey,* U.S. Office of Education (OE-25045) (Washington, D.C.: U.S. Government Printing Office, 1966).

3 Van Hoose and Vafakas, *op. cit.*

4 Willa Norris, "More Than a Decade of Training Guidance and Personnel Workers," *Personnel and Guidance Journal,* Vol. 39, No. 4 (December, 1960), pp. 287–91.

and Eckerson, however, about one third of the CDC's (child development consultants) were reported as having a background in psychology; teaching ranked second. Smith and Eckerson also found that about one fifth of the CDC's in their study were social workers. Thus, it can be concluded that most elementary school counselors are former teachers, while most CDC's are from psychology and social work.[5]

Financial Support

The great majority of elementary school counselors are supported in part by federal funds. The largest number of counselors are employed through funds from Title I, Elementary and Secondary Education Act. Less than one fourth are employed exclusively from state or local funds. Table 5 illustrates the number and percent of counselors employed under each category.

TABLE 5
Categories of Financial Support

	Elementary Counselors	
Financial Support	*Number*	*Percent*
Title V, NDEA	1,065	28
Title I, ESEA	1,372	37
State/local	860	22
Not classified	540	13
Total	3,837	100

State Standards

By 1967, 31 states and 1 territory had developed and published standards pertaining to guidance in the elementary school. For the most part, these standards are vague and lack specificity in terms of objectives and meeting desired changes in children. These statements provide general suggestions or recommendations on such matters as functions and qualifications of the counselor, organization of the guidance program, work with teachers, and physical facilities.[6]

This finding contrasts with an earlier study by Hill who found that only 15 states has published standards on guidance in the elementary school.[7] The expansion of Title V, National Defense Education Act, in 1964 has undoubtedly stimulated much effort toward developing standards for elementary school guidance. Several states have developed standards for program approval under National

[5] Smith and Eckerson, *op. cit.*

[6] Van Hoose and Vafakas, *op. cit.*

[7] George E. Hill, "Elementary School Guidance: Criteria for Approval by State Department of Education," *Counselor Education and Supervision*, Vol. 2, No. 3 (Spring, 1963), pp. 137–43.

Defense Education Act only. Table 6 shows the type of standards developed thus far.

TABLE 6

STATUS OF STATE STANDARDS FOR ELEMENTARY SCHOOL GUIDANCE

	States		*Territories*	
Type of Standard	*Number*	*Percent*	*Number*	*Percent*
NDEA only	13	25	1	25
State only	10	20		
State and NDEA	8	16		
Total	31	61	1	25

CERTIFICATION

In 1962, Arbuckle reported that none of the states had certification for counselors at the elementary level.[8] Roeber, in 1963, revealed that although there continued to be a lack of specific plans for elementary school counselor certification, nine states had implied elementary certification plans with no distinction from plans at the secondary level.[9] By 1964, two or three states were reported as having certification standards for elementary school counselors which were different from secondary standards.[10]

The 1967 survey reveals that 14 states have developed certification requirements for elementary school counselors which are discernably different from secondary certification. Two additional states have an endorsement procedure with specific requirements for counselors at the elementary level. Seven states are reported to be developing special plans for elementary certification, while the remaining number certify counselors in K-12.

The major distinctions which are made in certification requirements for elementary school counselors are mandatory teaching experience in the elementary school, and courses in child development, and counseling practicum. Two states having elementary certification indicate that a master's degree in elementary school guidance is required.[11] Table 7 illustrates the range of certification requirements in the several states.

---

8 Dugald S. Arbuckle, *Pupil Personnel Services in American Schools* (Boston: Allyn and Bacon, Inc., 1962).

9 Edward C. Roeber, *The School Counselor* (New York: Center for Applied Research in Education, 1963).

10 Herman J. Peters, Bruce Shertzer, and William H. Van Hoose, *Guidance in Elementary Schools* (Chicago: Rand McNally & Co., 1965), p. 246.

11 Van Hoose and Vafakas, *op. cit.*

TABLE 7

Certification Requirements for Elementary Counseling*

State	*Elem. Couns. Cert.*	*Elem. & Sec. Couns. Cert.*	*No Elem. Cert.*	*Type & Number of Couns. Cert. Provided*	*Teach. Cert. Required*	*Yrs. Teach. Exp. Required*	*Yrs. Couns. Exp. Required*	*Yrs. Work Exp. Required*	*Academic Preparation*	*University Recommendation Required*	*Other*
Alabama	...	X	...	Prof. A	X	2	...	...	M.A. inc. 18 hrs. in G. &. C.	...	...
				Prof. AA	...	...	X	...	M.A. + 30 hrs. in G. & C. or 6th yr. prog.		
Alaska	...	X	...	Limited	X	1	...	1	9 hrs. in G. & C.	...	...
				Prov.	...	2	...	1	18–24 hrs. in G. & C.		
				Maximum	...	2	1	1	24 hrs. in G. & C.		
Arizona	...	X	...	...	X	3	...	...	M.A. inc. 30 hrs. in G. & C.	...	...
Arkansas	X	...	...	...	...	...	...	...	M.A. in G. & C. (Elem.)	X	(C)
California	...	...	X	...	...	...	...	...	...	...	...
Colorado	X (A)	...	...	Perm. (E)	X	2	...	1	M.A. in G. & C.	...	...
Connecticut	X	...	...	Prov.	X	3	...	...	M.A. in G. & C. (Elem.)	X	...
				Standard	...	...	3	...			
Delaware	...	...	...	(B)	...	...	...	...	...	...	...
Florida	...	...	X	...	...	...	...	...	...	...	...
Georgia	...	X	...	(B)	...	...	...	...	...	...	...
Hawaii	...	X	...	Prof.	X	2	...	1	30 hrs. in G. & C.	...	(C)
Idaho	...	X	...	Interim	X	2	...	...	B.A. + 9 hrs. in G. & C.	...	...
				Standard	...	...	...	...	M.A. inc. 18 hrs. G. & C.		
Illinois	X	...	...	Prof.	X†	2†	...	...	Guid. Spec. Cert. or training in G. & C.	...	...
Indiana	...	...	X	...	...	...	...	...	...	...	...
Iowa	X	...	...	...	X†	2†	... (F)	...	M.A. in G. & C.	X	...

TABLE 7—Continued

CERTIFICATION REQUIREMENTS FOR ELEMENTARY COUNSELING*

State	Elem. Couns. Cert.	Elem. & Sec. Couns. Cert.	No Elem. Cert.	Type & Number of Couns. Cert. Provided	Teach. Cert. Required	Yrs. Teach. Exp. Required	Yrs. Couns. Exp. Required	Yrs. Work Exp. Required	Academic Preparation	University Recommendation Required	Other
Kansas	X	...	...	Standard	X†	2†	2†	...	M.A. in G. & C.	X	...
				Prof.	...	...	...	...	M.A. + 15 hrs. in G. & C.		
Kentucky	...	X	...	Prov.	X	3	...	...	M.A. in G. & C.	...	...
				Standard	...	2	...	1	M.A. + 24 hrs. in G. & C.		
Louisiana	...	...	X	...	...	...	...	...	...	...	...
Maine	X	...	...	Prov.	X†	2†	...	...	M.A. in G. & C.	...	...
				Prof.			3†				
Maryland	X	...	...	...	(G) X†	2†	2 (F)	...	Teach. cert. or M.A. in G. & C.	...	(H)
Massachusetts	X	...	...	...	X†	...	...	...	B.A. 12 hrs. in G. & C.	...	...
Michigan	...	...	X	...	...	...	...	...	...	...	...
Minnesota	...	...	X	...	...	...	...	...	...	...	...
Mississippi	...	X	...	Permit	X	1	...	...	12 hrs. in G. & C.	...	...
				Cert.		2	2 (F)		M.A. in G. & C.	...	(C)
Missouri	X	...	...	Minimum	X†	2	...	...	Training in G. & C.	...	...
				Maximum	...	2	...	...	M.A. in G. & C.	...	...
				Prof.	...	...	3	...	M.A. + 15 hrs. in G. & C.	...	...
Montana	(A) X	...	...	(E)	...	...	...	...	20 hrs. in G. & C.	X	...
Nebraska	...	...	X	...	...	...	...	...	...	...	...
Nevada	(A) X	...	...	Stand.	X†	1†	...	...	12 hrs. in G. & C.	...	...
				Prof.	...	2†	...	...	24 hrs. in G. & C.	...	...
New Hampshire	...	X	...	Pt. Time	X (G)	...	...	...	12 hrs. in G. & C.	...	...
				Full Tm.	...	2	...	...	M.A. in G. & C.	...	...
New Jersey	...	X	...	...	X	1	...	...	M.A. or 30 hrs. in G. & C.	...	...
New Mexico	...	X	...	(B)	...	...	...	...	...	...	...
New York	...	X	...	(B)	...	...	...	...	...	...	...

TABLE 7—Continued

CERTIFICATION REQUIREMENTS FOR ELEMENTARY COUNSELING*

State	*Elem. Couns. Cert.*	*Elem. & Sec. Couns. Cert.*	*No Elem. Cert.*	*Type & Number of Couns. Cert. Provided*	*Teach. Cert. Required*	*Yrs. Teach. Exp. Required*	*Yrs. Couns. Exp. Required*	*Yrs. Work Exp. Required*	*Academic Preparation*	*University Recommendation Required*	*Other*
North Carolina	...	...	X	...	...	...	...	...	...	...	...
North Dakota	...	X (D)	...	Stand.	X	2	...	1	15 hrs. in G. & C.	...	(C)
				Prof.	...	...	...	...	24 hrs. in G. & C.	X	...
Ohio	...	X	...	Minimum	X	1	...	1	M.A. in G. & C.	X	...
				Prof.	...	...	2	...	M.A. + ?? hrs. in G. & C.	...	...
				Perm.	...	...	4	...	M.A. + 9 hrs. in G. & C.	...	...
Oklahoma	X	...	...	(B)	...	...	...	...	...	...	...
Oregon	...	X	...	Basic	X	2	...	...	24 quarter hrs. G. & C.	...	...
				Stand.	...	...	2	...	48 quarter hrs. G. & C.	...	...
Pennsylvania	...	X	...	Prov.	(G) X	(I) X	...	...	18 hrs. in G. & C.	...	...
				Perm.	...	...	3	...	M.A.	...	...
Rhode Island	...	X	...	Prov.	...	3	...	1	15 hrs. in G. & C.	...	...
				Prof.	...	...	3	...	M.A. or B.A. + 36 hrs. in G. & C.	...	(J)
S. Carolina	X	...	...	...	X	2†	...	...	M.A. inc. 21–24 hrs. G. & C.	...	...
S. Dakota	...	X	...	Pt. Time	X	1	...	...	B.A. + 15 hrs. in G. & C.	...	...
				Full Tm.	...	...	...	...	M.A. in G. & C.	...	...
Tennessee	...	...	X	...	...	...	...	...	...	...	...
Texas	...	X	...	(B)	...	...	...	...	...	...	...
Utah	X	...	...	...	X†	2†	...	...	M.A. or 55 quarter hrs. in G. & C.	X	...
Vermont	...	X	...	...	X	...	...	1	15 hrs. G. & C.	X	...
Virginia	...	...	X	...	...	...	...	...	...	...	...
Washington	...	...	X	...	...	...	...	...	...	...	...

TABLE 7—Continued

CERTIFICATION REQUIREMENTS FOR ELEMENTARY COUNSELING*

State	Elem. Couns. Cert.	Elem. & Sec. Couns. Cert.	No Elem. Cert.	Type & Number of Couns. Cert. Provided	Teach. Cert. Required	Yrs. Teach. Exp. Required	Yrs. Couns. Exp. Required	Yrs. Work Exp. Required	Academic Preparation	University Recommendation Required	Other
W. Virginia	X	...	...	Endorsement	X†	...	...	...	12 hrs. in G. & C.	...	...
				Cert.	...	2	...	...	M.A. inc. 30 hrs. in G. & C.	...	...
Wisconsin		X	...	Grade B	X	2	...	1	B.A. inc. 18 hrs. in G. & C.	...	...
				Grade A	...	...	2	...	M.A. inc. 24 hrs. in G. & C.	...	...
Wyoming		X (A)	...	Initial	X	2	...	...	M.A. in G. & C. or Approved prog.	...	...
				Stand.	...	...	2	...	...	...	...
				Prof.	...	...	5	...	M.A. + 30 hrs.	...	...
Dist. of Colum.		X	...	...	...	(I) 2	...	...	M.A. inc. 30 hrs. in G. & C.	...	...
Canal Zone		...	X	...	...	...	...	...	...	...	...
Guam		...	X	...	...	...	...	...	...	...	...
Puerto Rico		...	X	...	...	...	...	...	...	...	...
Virgin Islands	X	...	...	Prov.	X	1	...	...	B.A.	...	...
				Perm.	...	...	...	...	M.A. inc. 30 hrs. in G. & C.	...	...

* When more than one type of certificate is issued, requirements for the second or third type of certificate are in addition to the requirements on the minimum certificate.

† At the elementary level.

(A) Counselor endorsement.

(B) Requirements not described.

(C) Practicum required.

(D) Counselor credential.

(E) Will issue counselor endorsement on three types of teaching certificates:
- Class 1. partially completed program in elementary education.
- Class 2. completed program in elementary education.
- Class 3. 3 years' teaching experience, B.A. + 1 year academic work.

(F) Teaching or counseling experience required.

(G) Desired, not required.

(H) Course in reading methods if no teaching experience.

(I) Experience in any educational field.

(J) Course in Rhode Island Education.

SUMMARY

Although the guidance movement at the elementary level has proceded some distance in the past few years, the number of schools with elementary *counselors* is still relatively small. While counselors continue to be employed for elementary schools at an accelerating rate, it will be several years before the majority of elementary schools in this country have the services of a counselor.

Almost 70 percent of the 3,837 elementary school counselors employed in 1967 were supported in part by federal funds. The majority of these counselors are former elementary teachers.

Some progress is evident in matters pertaining to certification for elementary school counselors. Fourteen states have developed certification requirements and seven additional states claim to have such requirements in process. The key differences between elementary and secondary school counselor certification in the above cases center on child development and the counseling practicum.

As noted above, only 31 states and 1 territory have developed standards for elementary school guidance. From this group, 13 states have developed standards and criteria only for approval of National Defense Education Act programs. One must assume then that much remains to be done in this area and further, that at the present time many programs are either experimental in nature or that they are operating without any direction from the state.

Finally, while there is definitely an upward trend in elementary school guidance, the movement has not yet reached ground swell proportions. There is still some confusion and movement in uncharted directions. Much of this confusion is the result of "growing pains," and the sincere desire to provide immediate services to boys and girls.

The question of whether we should have counselors in elementary schools is no longer pertinent. We cannot afford to be without them.

SELECTED REFERENCES

HILL, GEORGE E. "Elementary School Guidance: Criteria for Approval by State Department of Education," *Counselor Education and Supervision,* Vol. 2, No. 3 (Spring, 1963), pp. 137–43.

ROEBER, EDWARD C. *The School Counselor.* New York: Center for Applied Research in Education, 1963.

SMITH, HYRUM, and ECKERSON, LOUISE O. *Guidance Services in Elementary Schools: A National Survey,* U.S. Office of Education (OE-25045) Washington, D.C.: U.S. Government Printing Office, 1966.

VAN HOOSE, WILLIAM, and VAFAKAS, CATHERINE M. "Status of Guidance and Counseling in the Elementary School," *Personnel and Guidance Journal,* Vol. 46 (February, 1967), pp. 536–39.

Appendixes

A.

AN ELEMENTARY SCHOOL COUNSELOR'S SEMESTER IN REVIEW

By John Michael Murphy and Sandra Gokel Stewart

B.

STANDARDS FOR THE PREPARATION OF ELEMENTARY SCHOOL COUNSELORS

APPENDIX A

AN ELEMENTARY SCHOOL COUNSELOR'S SEMESTER IN REVIEW

By John Michael Murphy and Sandra Gokel Stewart

This paper describes the initiation and operation of the elementary school counseling program in the Fitzgerald School District. The district is comprised of four elementary schools with a total enrollment of 2,800 students and one combined junior-senior high school with a student population of approximately 2,200 students.

BACKGROUND

Covering an area of approximately four square miles, the Fitzgerald School District is located in the southwest corner of the city of Warren, which is a suburb located at the northern boundary of Detroit, Michigan. The automobile industry and its auxiliaries provide much of the economic framework for the school district. The residential areas vary from low- to medium-priced homes, of which 92 percent are privately owned. The occupations of the parents range from unskilled workers to a majority of semiskilled and skilled employees of the industrial complex within and surrounding the district.

Over a period of years, the principals within the district met as members of the Principals' Advisory Council. The council discussed individual student problems, school philosophy, and curriculum innovations. The members became aware of the need for early identification of difficulties youngsters experienced. They also began discussing research which suggested that dropouts could be identified at an early age. These discussions revealed the need for a guidance program at the elementary school level. Members of the council who were from the secondary level, aware that youngsters came to them from the lower grades with problems, provided the impetus for the studies which made this need clear to all concerned.

When a former member of the council became the new superintendent of schools, he presented a platform of ideas which would strengthen the elementary school program within the Fitzgerald District. A pilot program in elementary school counseling approved by the Board of Education resulted from his presentation.

A committee was appointed, comprised of the four elementary school principals and the Supervisor of Elementary Education, to screen applicants for the position of elementary school counselor. The Board of

Education then approved the selection recommended by the screening committee.

Within a few days, the new counselor met with the Supervisor of Elementary Education and with the principal of the school in which he would be located to discuss the role of the counselor as it related to administration. It was emphasized that the counselor is not a teacher, an administrator, or a disciplinarian. It was agreed at that time that the counselor would be directly responsible to the Supervisor of Elementary Education, but his immediate supervisor would be the principal of the building.

At this time, the counselor was shown the facilities available for his services. These consisted of an office, a counselor's desk and chair, a filing cabinet, and a bookshelf. The office is easily accessible from the main corridor of the building, and is not located near the principal's office. Crayons, pencils, and paper are available for use by the children. Also, there are cork strips on the wall which can be used to display any drawings or other articles which the child may desire.

Defining Roles

A meeting to establish a relationship between the school social worker and counselor defined the role of each and how cooperation and consultation between them would offer a team approach. The school social worker is concerned with the extreme social or emotional problems that impede a child's achievement. The social worker works with parents, children, school, and community personnel. The case load of the social worker is comprised of referrals which are screened, selected, and periodically evaluated. When there is a need, the child may receive support from the counselor, even though he is a social worker referral. Ultimately, the relationship between the school social worker and the counselor should be flexible enough to shift emphasis according to the needs expressed in individual situations.

In comparison, the elementary school counselor is concerned with *all* children. No child's problem is too minor for the elementary school counselor. If the child regards it as a problem, the counselor regards it as a problem. The emphasis is upon prevention, with the intent that the child will be helped to cope with any developmental, social, or emotional difficulties before they become severe. Basically, the counselor is helping the child learn to solve his own problems. The counselor's office is like a mental health first-aid station to which a child may go at any time. This means that referrals to the elementary school counselor may come from many sources—from teachers, parents, administrators, other school personnel, and from the child himself. The counselor is also a consultant for teachers, administrators, and parents.

A discussion among the school psychological examiner, the director of special education, and the counselor revealed ways in which the counselor might be of some assistance to the school psychological examiner.

In the state of Michigan, the school psychological examiner is licensed to provide individual testing and to certify for the program for mentally retarded and/or for the special education program. In the Fitzgerald District, the psychological examiner is in charge of the entire testing program in the elementary school, including group testing (California Test of Mental Maturity and the California Achievement Tests). It was thought at this time that the counselor might be helpful in administering the group tests in his school to ensure proper administration. The counselor was not enthusiastic about assuming this responsibility, but agreed to due so reluctantly.

It is important to note at this time that, although the administration was responsible for gaining approval of the program, the counselor was given a free hand to establish the kind of program which he deemed appropriate. He believed that the main emphasis of the program should be upon individual counseling. The child's self-concept was to be the main concern of the counselor during the counseling session, meaning that the counselor would attempt to help the child gain a better understanding of himself and his life-space.

Some of the goals of the counseling program included:

1. The elementary school counselor should be available to help *all* children who need special help, in order that they may better achieve their potential in the school situation and ultimately become productive and worthwhile citizens. The type of help provided varies according to the need.

2. The elementary school counselor should work with chilmunity agencies to achieve these ends.

3. The elementary school counselor should serve as the central agent in his particular school to facilitate referrals to special services and community agencies. This includes those who need help for emotional, psychological, mental, physical, or economic reasons.

4. The elementary school counselor shall interpret to the teacher, parent, and child the results of any tests administered to gain more understanding of the child, except those administered by the school diagnostician.

5. In order to attempt to meet the needs of all the children, the school system should know very early the pupils who are

exceptional, either at one extreme or the other. The counselor should have primary responsibility for early identification of these children and help advise on methods and curriculum to meet their needs.

6. The counselor should be the consultant in the school building for the promotion of good mental health practices. This includes possible in-service training for teachers and administrators if deemed advisable, as well as a source of help for parents.

7. The elementary school counselor should be the liaison between the elementary school and the junior and the senior high school counselors. This means there must be communication and cooperation among all counselors.

It is probably quite apparent that the above goals are of a continuing nature. They are never attained once and for all, but rather must always be sought and resought.

Getting Started

A few days prior to assuming his new duties, the counselor attended a faculty meeting at the school in which the counseling program was to begin. The school, kindergarten through sixth grade, had an enrollment at this time of approximately 820 children with a faculty of 30 teachers. At this meeting the counselor explained briefly the role of the counselor, the purposes of counseling, and the need for cooperation by all concerned. It was emphasized that the counselor was to be available for *all* children. The counselor requested that the teachers first send the counselor some of their best pupils to get acquainted and possibly avoid any stigma that might be associated with visiting the counselor.

A few days after the meeting with the faculty, the second semester of the school year began. That day and part of the following day the counselor went to each room, introduced himself, explained briefly the purpose of the new counseling program, and answered questions. The children would then know him upon sight, and he would not be a stranger to any who might come for his services. The counselor did not want to be introduced by the principal, in order to avoid any possible link with administration in the minds of the children or of the teachers.

In talking about the new program, the counselor emphasized that there were many people in the school who were there only to help the children, for example, teachers, principal, nurse, and speech therapist. He explained that sometimes teachers and other school personnel do not have sufficient time to discuss with each child some concerns that the child might have, but that he would be available for that purpose.

Some of the possible concerns mentioned by the counselor included: personal dissatisfaction with school achievement or with peer relations, loneliness, fears, or the need to express emotions openly.

The confidentiality of the counseling session was also stressed. One of the difficulties of this task was to express these concepts in terminology appropriate to the grade level of the children. At all times the counselor stressed the positive nature of counseling; that it was an opportunity to obtain guidance over some of the hurdles of life.

The First Week

On the second day after beginning his new duties, the counselor received his first referral, a fifth-grade boy. His teacher discussed with the counselor some of the problems she was having with this boy. Later that day the counselor had his first counseling session with this counselee.

The next day, the principal of the school and the counselor visited another school district, in which an elementary counseling program had been started a semester before. They discussed the aims and procedures of this program with the Director of Personnel in that district, who had been instrumental in helping to plan their program. There were many similarities between the procedures used in the two programs. In the other school district, however, there were four counselors, which necessitated some coordination, meetings, and reporting that were not needed at Fitzgerald.

Later that day, the counselor held individual counseling sessions with eight sixth-graders, who had referred themselves mainly out of curiosity.

The following day, nine counseling sessions were held. Before the first week ended, the counselor had held 24 counseling sessions, conferred with one mother, who referred her son to the counselor, and consulted with three teachers.

Since this program was new, it seemed appropriate to maintain a daily log of the counselor's activities. This was done voluntarily by the counselor with the expectation that it might be useful in any future evaluation.

The following is a duplication of a week's activities as counselor:

Daily Log

Week Ending March 18

Monday, March 14	– Conducted six counseling sessions. Held parent-teacher conference. Met with parent, teacher, psychological examiner, and principal. Prepared Daily Activity Sheet. Worked on card catalog.
Tuesday, March 15	– Conducted nine counseling sessions. Wrote letter to a physician to obtain information concerning a counselee. Prepared Daily Activity Sheet.
Wednesday, March 16	– Conducted seven counseling sessions. Wrote report regarding the Elementary School Counseling Workshop at East Lansing, Michigan. Prepared Daily Activity Sheet.
Thursday, March 17	– Conducted seven counseling sessions. Began work on filing system. Prepared Daily Activity Sheet.
Friday, March 18	– Conducted six counseling sessions. Conference with one teacher. Conference with one parent. Contacted Children's Aid and Family Service. Worked on filing system. Prepared Daily Activity Sheet.

Working with Children

From the beginning, it was hoped that this new program would be accepted as worthwhile by the children and by the teachers, since they are regarded as the most important factors in the learning process. During the first week, 16 referrals were made by the teachers and 8 by the children themselves. The initial interview was used by the counselor for the purpose of establishing the type of rapport that would help make future contacts fruitful. Much of the first contact was spent in gathering factual information, such as name, address, telephone number, facts about the family, and making the counselee comfortable in the counseling session. The nature of the counseling session and its confidentiality also was explained. It was also stressed that during the counseling session the counselee is free to do or to say whatever he wishes. Before he left, each counselee was asked if he would be willing to return for future sessions. This was done for the purpose of emphasizing the fact that, in order for the counseling session to be effective, there must be a desire on the part of the counselee to participate. During the remainder of the first year, no one refused; in fact, just the opposite became apparent. Most counselees asked to see the counselor more often than was practicable.

As the year progressed, referrals came from parents, the principal, the school nurse, and the teachers. It soon became obvious that most referrals represented learning, social, or behavior problems. This was especially true of the counselees in the upper elementary grades.

It had been hoped in the beginning that more emphasis could be placed on the developmental difficulties which some children may experience. Instead, most of the time of the counselor seemed to be spent with the type of problems mentioned above. In order to attempt to counteract this tendency, the counselor, at various times during the year, invited lower grade classes to come to visit him to draw pictures, and to become acquainted. Many of these children then began coming to the counselor's office at the end of the school day, just to visit. It seemed that they looked upon the counselor as a special kind of helper.

During the third week of the program, the counselor gave the California Achievement Tests to grades four through six over the public address system. This was done at the direction of the administration. The counselor was apprehensive as to what effect this might have concerning his image in the minds of the children. He had been trying to emphasize that he was nonauthoritative and nonjudgmental. While he did not appear personally in the various classrooms, all the children who took the test knew the counselor was administering it. The counselor feels his apprehension was justified. Some of the comments of the children afterward included:

"I was surprised to hear your voice over the P. A. system."

"Why did you have to give the test?"

In the beginning, an attempt was made for the counselor to categorize the types of problems of the counselees. This was discontinued very early. The reason was that it became apparent that it was an impossible task to classify these problems. Learning problems frequently were behavior problems, and it would be necessary to make a complete and thorough diagnosis of each counselee, which is not the task of the counselor.

Working with Teachers and Administrators

From the beginning it was apparent that the counselor would have to devise some means for keeping records. The first form prepared is the Referral to Elementary School Counselor on which the person initiating the referral may include pertinent information including name, date, grade, and teacher, most convenient time for the child to leave his room, and any comments which the referring person may wish to make.

Another form used by the counselor is a request for the child to come to the counselor at a specified time. It is usually placed in the teacher's mailbox the morning of the day of the proposed counseling session.

The third form is used for the purpose of initiating a meeting with a teacher for consultation concerning a counselee.

The important consideration in arranging the counseling sessions and the meetings with teachers has been the convenience of the teachers so that interference with classroom activities may be minimal.

One of the concerns of the administrators was that they should be kept informed as to what is happening in the building. The following procedures were instituted to meet this need. A form called Daily Counseling Activity is filled out at the end of each day in triplicate. This form contains the name of each counselee for that particular day, grade level, time of the counseling session, source of original referral, and the total number of contacts for each counselee. Also, on this form the counseling sessions that have been held by the counselor since the beginning of the year are numbered consecutively, so that at the end of each day the number of counseling sessions for the year is apparent. One copy of this form is sent to the principal at the end of each day, another goes to the Supervisor of Elementary Education, and the third is filed in the counselor's office.

Another means of informing administration of the counselor's activities is a 4 x 6 index card that is made out for each counselee. On this card is written the counselee's name, counselee number, grade, teacher, address, telephone, and birth date. The date of the original referral is noted, as well as the date of the initial interview and each contact after that. These cards are kept in a card file that is available to the principal at all times, even when the counselor might not be present. In this way, the principal is able to determine, if needed, the number of counseling sessions for any particular counselee. Because of the confidential nature of the counseling session, however, there is no information available to anyone, other than the counselor. Only he knows what is discussed or what transpires. Any notes which the counselor may write concerning the counseling session are kept in a locked file, to which only the counselor has access.

Another form which the counselor found necessary is the Counselor Record Sheet. This consists of a list of the counselees, with each one numbered consecutively, so that at any time, the number of counselees who have come to the counselor is known. This form has a square for each week of the school year, so that the counselor can determine quickly if many weeks have passed without a counseling session for a particular counselee.

Consulting with Parents

It became obvious very early that many of the problems which became apparent in school stem from home conditions. For this reason, the counselor frequently asked parents to come to school for a conference. Many of these conferences were held in the evening in order to make it more convenient for fathers to attend. The purpose of these meetings in most cases was to share information concerning the child and then to arrive at some tentative program of action that could be followed at home and in school. A few times other school personnel took part in these conferences. The counselor did not make any home visits. This is primarily one of the functions of the school social worker.

Consultations with teachers were held at various times; sometimes before contact was made with the counselee, and at least once after enough contacts had been made for the counselor to make some contribution to the meeting.

Frequently the principal of the school would request the counselor's presence at a meeting with parents in his office. This served two purposes. It frequently became the source of a referral to the counselor, and the principal was making full use of the services of the counselor. Also, during the year the principal would confer with the counselor concerning the problems of individual children. In turn the counselor would share with the principal some of his findings concerning some of the counselees, providing it would not endanger the confidentiality of the counseling session.

Working with the Community

There were no formal referrals made by the counselor to any other service or community agency during this period. The counselor concurred in the referral of one child to the school social worker, which was made by the principal. Also, the parents of one child were aided by the counselor in acquiring the services of a child psychologist, and two other parents were informed about the services offered by the Child Guidance Clinic and by the Children's Aid and Family Service.

The Salvation Army was contacted by the counselor, and he was informed about the welfare services that this organization provides. The counselor also made contact, during this period, with the County Youth Home and the County Juvenile Court Probation Officer on behalf of two boys who were having difficulties with the law.

SUMMARY

By the end of the year, a period of one semester, 145 children had been referred to the counselor. This represented 18 percent of the total school population. In addition, 169 kindergarten, first, and second graders came to visit the counselor in groups of four or five to get acquainted. This represented another 20 percent of the total enrollment. In all, the counselor made personal contact with 38 percent of the school population in his office.

Of the 145 counselees, 95 were teacher referrals (65 percent), 32 were self-referrals (22 percent), 10 were referred by parents (7 percent), 7 were referred by the principal (5 percent), and 1 referred by the Special Education Committee (less than 1 percent).

A further analysis shows that 40 percent of the counselees have come from the primary grades and that 60 percent originated from grades four through six.

There were three personal contacts with the seventh- and eighth-grade counselors during this period. The elementary school counselor attended a meeting of the junior and senior high school counselors in order to lay the groundwork for future cooperation.

An attempt has been made to present a factual, objective summary of the elementary school counseling program at Westview Elementary School in the Fitzgerald School District during its first year.

The counselor feels obliged to assert that this program was initiated under optimum conditions for its success. The impetus provided by the administration and the facilities provided were of the highest quality. The operation of the program was further enhanced by the cooperative spirit of the entire faculty, the school social worker, the school psychological examiner, the Special Education Department, and the parents. Of utmost importance also was the encouragement, understanding, and cooperation of the administration.

From the counselor's point of view, a very beneficial aspect of this program was the freedom given to him by administration. He was recognized as the expert in this area and was permitted to organize the elementary school counseling program without interference. In this way, he was able to make optimum use of the knowledge and understanding provided by his training and education.

APPENDIX B

STANDARDS FOR THE PREPARATION OF ELEMENTARY SCHOOL COUNSELORS

American Personnel and Guidance Association
Association for Counselor Education and Supervision

Section I. Philosophy and Objectives

1. The institution has a stated philosophy of education and has developed a set of objectives for counselor education consistent with that philosophy.
   a. Such statements have been prepared cooperatively by the staff members in counselor education.
   b. Such statements are in harmony with the institution's philosophy and objectives, have been accepted by the administration and are supported at the policy-making level.
   c. State and local guidance personnel and representatives from related disciplines (particularly those with elementary school experience) have been consulted in reviewing the institution's objectives for counselor education.
   d. The statements of philosophy and objectives are reflected in the institution's publications and programs.
   e. Philosophy and objectives are reflected in the attitude and behavior of staff and students in the program.
2. The objectives of the counselor education program were developed by a staff who are aware of the total school problem.
   a. The objectives reflect the staff's awareness of the uniqueness of the structures and settings of public and non-public school education in the country.
   b. Due consideration is given to developments and trends in school organization, curriculum, and program.
   c. The objectives include a recognition of the role of the elementary school counselor encouraging and facilitating desirable changes in education.
3. The staff continues to review the objectives of the program in the light of current conditions and research findings.
4. There is continuous study of the extent to which the stated philosophy is transmitted and the objectives are accomplished.
   a. There is a planned program for assessing changes in attitudes and behavior of students as they move through the counselor education program.

b. Flexibility of assignments and experiences is provided for students with differing backgrounds of preparation and experience.
c. Personnel in cooperating schools and agencies participate in the evaluation process on a formally recognized basis.
d. Evidence obtained from former students, data from the schools to which they are assigned, and information obtained by representatives of the state department of education are systematically used in evaluating the effectiveness of the elementary school counselor preparation program.

Section II. Curriculum: Program of Studies and Supervised Experiences

A. General Program Characteristics.

1. The institution provides a graduate program specifically designed for the preparation of elementary school counselors, based primarily on the program of studies and supervised practice outlined in B and C below. The length and content of the program varies with the student's undergraduate preparation but shall be a minimum of one year of graduate counselor education leading to a graduate degree. The institution provides at least one additional year of graduate study in counselor education either through its own staff and facilities or through cooperative working relationships with other institutions which do have at least a two-year program of counselor education.
   a. The opportunity for full-time study in counselor education is provided throughout the academic year.
   b. Flexibility is provided within the curriculum to allow for individual differences in competencies and understandings developed prior to entering the institution's counselor education program.
   c. The organized curriculum for the program is published and is available for distribution to prospective students. This description includes information relating to the institution's requirements for full-time study.
2. There is evidence of quality instruction in all aspects of the counselor education program.
   a. Syllabi or other evidences of organized and coordinated instructional units of the curriculum are available.
   b. Appropriate resource materials are provided.
   c. Responsibilities are assigned to or assumed by staff members only in those areas for which they are professionally qualified by preparation and experience.

d. Provisions are made for periodic evaluation by students, staff, former students and employers of all aspects of the counselor education program, such as course content, methods of instruction, and supervised experiences both on and off campus.
e. Evaluation is followed by appropriate revisions and improvements, if indicated.

3. Planned sequences of educational experiences are provided.
   a. A sequence of basic and advanced graduate courses and other associated learning experiences is defined and provided.
   b. The program provides for the integration of didactic instruction, seminars, and supervised experiences in counseling and other related guidance services throughout the sequence.
   c. Prerequisites are identified.
4. Cooperation exists among staff members directly responsible for the professional education of counselors and representatives of departments or schools offering courses in related fields.
   a. Cooperative working arrangements are in existence.
   b. Staff members from related areas meet with the counselor staff for planning, implementing and evaluating the counselor education program.
   c. Course work in other areas is identified for the counselor candidate with respect to its appropriateness for graduate credit or for background work.
   d. There is evidence of interdisciplinary planning with respect to both student and staff participation in designing, conducting, and evaluating research.
5. Within the framework of the total counselor education program, there are available curriculum resources as well as procedures that make it possible for the counselor candidate to develop understandings and skills beyond the minimum requirements of the program.
   a. Elective courses are available.
   b. Staff time is provided for the supervision of individual study in the areas of counselor education.
   c. Advisers make counselor candidates aware of such opportunities.
6. The counselor education staff encourages the spirit of inquiry and the production and use of research data.
   a. The statement of objectives of the program reflects an awareness of the role of research in the work of the counselor and the competencies to be developed.
   b. Instructional procedures make frequent use of, and reference

to, research findings. Areas in which research is needed are identified.

7. Opportunities for self-evaluation and the further development of self-understanding are provided for the counselor candidate.
   a. Opportunities are provided through such activities as laboratory experiences, supervised counseling, and self-analysis through tape recordings and/or video tapes.
   b. Opportunities for improvement of interpersonal relationships are provided through small group activities.
   c. Counseling services provided by persons other than the counselor education staff are available to students in counselor education.

B. Program of Studies.

1. The program of studies provides adequate preparation in education, the behavioral sciences, and the work of the elementary school counselor. Some of the topics listed below require more than one course to provide adequate preparation while others can be covered adequately as units in a course. Though elementary school counselors can be taught some of the core courses with other counselors, those counselors polled by the committee strongly recommend that certain courses in individual counseling techniques, group counseling and guidance techniques, and the practicum be taught in separate sections designed especially for elementary school counselors.
   a. Information on the educational setting is provided concerning the purposes and organization of the elementary school, school curriculum, and philosophy and sociology of schools.
   b. Work from the behavioral sciences is provided in child growth and development, personality dynamics and theories, dynamics of family living, group dynamics, and theories of learning.
   c. Professional studies in elementary school counseling are provided in the following topics:
      (1) Counseling theories and techniques
      (2) Group procedures in guidance and counseling
      (3) Professional identification, the profession, and its ethics
      (4) Role definition, program development, and coordination of elementary school guidance services
      (5) The consultation process
      (6) Individual appraisal
      (7) Vocational development theory, including the use of appropriate materials for elementary school children
      (8) Research skills to enable the elementary school counselor

to understand the relevant research and to appraise the outcomes of his services.

C. Supervised Experiences.

1. Supervised experiences in counseling and other guidance activities are provided as an integral part of the total counselor education program.
   a. Settings in which such experiences are provided are appropriate for the preparation of elementary school counselors.
   b. These supervised experiences, including both observation of and work directly with elementary school children, their parents and their teachers, frequently are provided in the actual school situation. Opportunities are provided for these prospective counselors to consult with parents, teachers, and other school personnel as well as to counsel pupils and parents.
   c. Opportunities are provided for working with a variety of elementary school and community agency personnel.
   d. All such experiences are conducted under established ethical policies.
   e. Primary responsibility for all supervised experiences is assigned to counselor education staff members qualified as stated in C3 below; qualified elementary school counselors and qualified advanced graduate students may be employed and assigned subsidiary responsibilities.
2. Three aspects of supervised experience are recognized in the counselor education program—laboratory experiences, practicum experiences, and internship.
   a. Laboratory experiences are provided in the first and/or second years.
      (1) Opportunities are provided for prospective elementary school counselors to observe and participate in activities related to the total guidance program; e.g., role-playing, listening to tapes, testing, organizing and using pupil personnel records, conducting case conferences, and working with professional personnel.
      (2) Laboratory experiences appropriate to the counselor candidate's needs are a continuing part of the counselor education program.
      (3) Plans and procedures adopted by the staff clearly describe the integration of such experiences.
   b. Practicum experiences are provided in the first and/or second years.
      (1) Practicum consists of consultation with teachers and par-

ents and counseling and small group work with pupils and parents.

(2) Practicum is conducted in settings which are appropriate for the preparation of elementary school counselors.

(3) Practicum includes opportunity for continuing experiences in a series of counseling relationships with varying types of elementary school children.

(4) A stated number of hours is spent by each counselor candidate in actual counseling relationships. This does not include time required for preparation and for supervisory consultations.

a. Counselor education students completing the two-year program spend 60 hours as a minimum.

b. Counselor education students completing a one-year program spend 30 hours as a minimum.

(5) Opportunity is provided within the total work load for staff to supervise practicum experiences.

(6) Media such as tape recorders, television and one-way vision screens are utilized in the supervision of the practicum activities.

(7) Practicum provides for a growth experience which is spread over a period of time.

(8) Supervised experiences are provided as an integral part of courses throughout the counselor education program of the student.

c. Internship may be provided. This is optional, though recommended.

(1) Internship is an advanced level of on-the-job supervised experience offered in an elementary school setting.

(2) It is under the systematic supervision of qualified members of both the school staff and the institution's counselor education staff.

(3) It is normally a paid experience.

(4) Opportunities are provided for the counselor candidate to share responsibilities in all phases of the school guidance program.

3. A well-qualified staff with adequate time allocated to supervision is provided.

a. Members of the on-campus staff responsible for supervision

(1) Have earned advanced degrees in a relevant academic field (preferably the doctorate) from accredited institutions.

(2) Have had experience in counseling and related guidance activities with elementary school children.

b. Elementary school staff members who supervise counselor candidates concurrently with the institution's staff should have at least two years of graduate work in counselor education or have equivalent preparation.

c. Doctoral students who supervise practicum experiences as a part of their preparation have appropriate advance graduate work and experience with elementary school children.

d. The counseling practicum is virtually a tutorial form of instruction; therefore, the supervision of five students is equivalent to the teaching of one three-semester-hour course. Such a ratio is considered maximum.

e. Supervision of internship is provided regularly by the cooperating elementary school staff and adequate staff time is allocated both for day-to-day supervision and for weekly supervisory conferences.

f. Supervisors from the institution's staff have internship consultations and supervision assigned as part of their total work load.

g. Time is allocated by the school system for elementary school staff members to assist in supervision of laboratory practicum, and internship experiences.

4. Appropriate facilities, equipment, and materials are provided for supervised experiences in both on-and-off campus settings. (See section IV.)

D. The institution assists cooperating school systems, state departments of education, and individual school counselors with activities which contribute to in-service growth and to the improvement of the school's guidance programs.

1. There is a planned means of communication to encourage school and pupil personnel administration to seek the institution's assistance in planning and conducting in-service education and program-improvement activities.

2. The institution's staff is provided load recognition for their part in in-service and program development activities in the schools.

3. The institution's staff in counselor education involves its graduate students in its in-service and program development activities in the schools as a means of enriching their experiences.

Section III. Selection, Retention, Endorsement, and Placement

1. The institution has a procedure for identifying and selecting candidates for counselor education.
   a. The counselor education staff has cooperatively developed criteria and procedures relating to selection, retention, endorsement, and placement.
   b. The criteria used for selection are consistent with the philosophy and objectives of the institution's counselor education program.
   c. Information about the counselor education program and about certification in the several states is available to the candidates.
   d. Qualified candidates may be drawn from various undergraduate fields and from various occupations.
      (1) Candidates who have been teachers have demonstrated superior potential for counseling in the elementary schools.
      (2) Candidates from fields other than teaching demonstrate their understanding of the elementary schools and their competence to perform guidance and counseling functions in elementary schools by completing courses and supervised experiences planned for this purpose.
      (3) Appraisal of a candidate's potential for counseling should be solicited from professors, employers, and state department personnel.
   e. Members of the counselor education staff are available to confer with prospective candidates.
2. The institution follows a defined procedure for the selective admission and retention of candidates.
   a. The candidate is assessed with respect to:
      (1) Potential for developing effective relationships with children, teachers, administrators, and parents.
      (2) Familiarity with themselves and the objectives of the program.
      (3) Capacity to to graduate work.
      (4) Potential for engaging in research.
   b. The counselor education staff admits to the program only those candidates who meet the requirements established for admission to study in counselor education. These requirements may be in addition to those established by the institution for admission to graduate study.
   c. Decisions with respect to admission to the counselor education program are made by the staff (or by a committee) and not by any one staff member. All candidates are informed that their con-

tinuation in the program is not automatic but is subject to periodic review.

3. The institution administers a planned program of selective retention, designating points within the program for evaluation of progress and informing of procedures for selective retention.
   a. The counselor education staff has the responsibility of denying continuation in the program to any candidate whose level of academic performance and/or personal characteristics do not adequately meet institutional or professional standards.
   b. Each counselor candidate is encouraged to enter into a program of self-evaluation related to his retention in the program. To assist him in his growth in self-understanding, a counseling service separate from the counselor education program is available to him.
   c. When appropriate, cooperating school counselors and state supervisors and administrators are consulted concerning decisions about retention of candidates.
   d. Decisions with respect to retention or dismissal of a candidate are made by the staff (or by a committee) and not by any one staff member.

4. The institution endorses successful candidates for certification and employment.
   a. A statement of policy relating to the institution's procedure for formal endorsement has been adopted by the staff and approved by the proper administrative authority.
   b. Each candidate is informed of procedures for endorsement for certification and employment.
   c. The counselor education staff participates in this endorsement procedure.
   d. Endorsement is given only on the basis of evidence of proficiency. This implies that the candidate has completed a substantial part of his graduate work in counselor education, including supervised counseling experience, at the endorsing institution, and that his personal growth is considered to have been satisfactory.

5. The institution provides a placement service.
   a. Placement service organization and procedures are consistent with established principles of student personnel work.
   b. Provision is made for the participation of personnel from the state department of education and cooperating schools in the placement of candidates and their induction into the profession.

c. Students are assisted as needed in the preparation of placement papers.
d. Staff members utilize individual professional relationships to assist in the placement of their graduates.
e. Assistance is provided in the evaluation of job opportunities and in the selection of positions appropriate to the individual's qualifications.
f. The placement service provides continuing assistance to the candidate throughout his professional career.

6. The institution maintains a program of research designed to evaluate its selection, retention, endorsement, and placement procedures.
   a. School counselors, administrators and state department of education personnel, when appropriate, participate in the planning and execution of the follow-up program and other evaluative procedures.
   b. The program of evaluation and follow-up includes early leavers as well as those who complete the program.
   c. Evaluation is followed by appropriate revisions and improvements.

SECTION IV. SUPPORT FOR THE COUNSELOR EDUCATION PROGRAM, ADMINISTRATIVE RELATIONS AND INSTITUTIONAL RESOURCES

1. Administrative organization and procedures provide recognition of and designated responsibilities for a counselor education program.
   a. The program is a clearly identified part of an institutional graduate program.
      (1) There is a designated unit responsible for the preparation of school counselors.
      (2) The program is oriented toward and administered through the unit responsible for graduate work in education.
   b. Cooperative relationships exist between the counselor education program and other units of the institution related to the program.
      (1) Contributions of other units to the program are defined.
      (2) Channels of communication with staff members in other units are identified and maintained.
   c. Use is made of a wide range of professional and community resources.
      (1) Sound working relations exist with state departments of education, public and private schools, community agencies and professional organizations.
      (2) Effective use is made of a wide variety of resource materials and personnel.

2. The institution provides for the professional development of the staff as well as students in the counselor education program.
   a. Staff members are active in professional leadership and research on a local, state, regional and national level.
   b. Staff members are participating in voluntary professional service capacities.
   c. Staff members engage in programs of research and contribute to the literature of the field.
   d. The institution provides encouragement and financial support for the staff to participate in such professional activities.
   e. The program exemplifies high professional standards in all relationships to students.
   f. Students learn about and participate in the activities of professional organizations.
3. The institution provides adequate faculty and staff for all aspects of the counselor education program.
   a. An individual is designated as the responsible professional leader of the counselor education program.
      (1) This individual is an experienced counselor and possesses an earned doctorate from an accredited institution in counselor education, or a closely related area.
      (2) This individual has a primary and preferably a full-time assignment to the counselor education program.
      (3) This individual's other responsibilities are consistent with and supportive of his primary obligations to the program of counselor education.
      (4) This individual is recognized for his leadership and service activities in the profession.
      (5) This individual is qualified by preparation and experience to conduct or to supervise research activities.
   b. A minimum basic staff includes the equivalent of at least three full-time qualified persons whose primary assignment is in counselor education, to insure staff depth to carry out curricular responsibilities of the professional studies and of the supervised practice and to provide program advisory service and supervision of research. Any institution which prepares elementary school counselors must have at least one qualified specialist in elementary school counseling who works full-time in his specialty.
      (1) In addition to the designated leader of the staff this includes at least the equivalent of two full-time faculty members with qualifications comparable to those of the chairman, or director, of the counselor education program.

(2) Additional basic staff members are provided in a ratio of approximately the equivalent of one full-time staff member for every eight full-time graduates or their equivalent in part-time graduate students.

(3) The full-time reaching load of these staff members is consistent with that of other graduate departments in the institution.

(4) This load is modified in proportion to assigned responsibilities for graduate advisement and research supervision on some formula which is consistent with established graduate school policy in the institution.

(5) Time is provided within the total work load for cooperative interdisciplinary activity with staff members in related fields.

(6) The total work load of staff members includes a recognition of time needed for professional research.

c. Faculty in related disciplines are qualified in their respective areas and also are informed about the objectives of counselor education.

d. Off-campus school personnel who supervise counselor candidates are qualified through academic preparation and professional experience.

(1) A basic policy provides for the identification, recognition and compensation of these staff members as an integral part of the counselor education staff.

(2) Such staff members have two or more years of appropriate professional experience.

(3) These staff members have at least two years of graduate work in elementary school counselor preparation or have equivalent preparation.*

e. Graduate assistantships are provided to reduce routine demands on staff and to provide additional experiences to students in the program.

(1) Regular procedures are established for the identification and assignment of qualified students to these assistantships.

(2) These assignments are made in such a way as to enrich the professional learning experiences of the graduate assistants.

f. Adequate secretarial and clerical staff is provided in the counselor education program.

(1) Clerical responsibilities are defined and responsibility for supervision of clerical staff is clearly identified.

* While the committee realizes that few elementary school counselors have this preparation today, this standard represents a reasonable expectation for the near future.

(2) A minimum of one full-time secretary is provided for the clerical work of the counselor education program.
(3) Additional clerical service is provided on a ratio of approximately one full-time clerical assistant for every three faculty members.

4. For the counselor education program the institution provides facilities and a budget which are sufficient to insure continuous operation of all aspects of the program.
   a. The institution provides a designated headquarters for the counselor education program.
      (1) This headquarters is located near the classroom and laboratory facilities used in the counselor education program.
      (2) The headquarters area includes well-equipped private offices for all professional staff members.
      (3) The headquarters area includes office space for clerical staff and graduate assistants.
   b. Practicum facilities are provided on and/or off campus in cooperating schools or other agencies.
      (1) These facilities include an adequate number of counseling offices.
      (2) Facilities are equipped with recording and listening devices for observation and supervision.
      (3) One-way vision screens are located in such a way as to provide for observation by an individual or by a whole class.
      (4) If the institution has closed-circuit television facilities, these are available to the program of counselor education.
      (5) Conference rooms are provided for tape analysis and small group conferences.
      (6) Portable recorders are available in sufficient numbers.
      (7) Seminar rooms are provided.
      (8) Ample and appropriate audio-visual and demonstration materials are available for staff and student use.
      (9) A variety of resource material is available for the demonstration and use of current information services in elementary school.
   c. Library facilities provide a rich supply of resource materials for both research and study in counselor education.
      (1) These include basic resources, both books and periodicals in elementary education, child growth and development, elementary school guidance, counseling, personality, psychology, sociology, social work, economics and other related disciplines.
      (2) Both current and historical materials are available.

(3) Library resources are available during both evening and week-end hours.

(4) Inter-library loans, microfilm and photocopy services are available.

(5) Multiple copies of frequently used publications are available.

d. Guidance and counseling center facilities are utilized on and/or off campus for the supervised experiences.

(1) Opportunities are provided for both observation and participation.

(2) These facilities provide for a broad variety of types and levels of experience and thus provide an understanding of a wide range of professional guidance and counseling activities both in and out of the elementary school setting.

e. Testing laboratory facilities are available.

(1) Files of tests and test interpretation data are available.

(2) Space for both group and individual testing is provided.

(3) Students have access to test scoring equipment.

f. Research facilities are available to both staff and students in counselor education.

(1) Facilities include offices and laboratories equipped to provide opportunities for collection, analysis and summary of data.

(2) Consultant services are available from research specialists on the institution's staff.

(3) Calculators are provided in these offices for research work.

(4) Access is provided to campus computer centers and other data processing laboratories.

(5) Settings are provided in which research can be conducted, including campus laboratories and elementary schools which provide enabling relationships to students and staff in counselor education.

5. The institution recognizes the individual needs of graduate students and provides services for personal as well as professional development.

a. Since full-time academic-year attendance is possible for most graduate students only if some form of financial assistance is available, every effort is made to develop appropriate assistantships and fellowships in counselor education.

(1) The counselor education program is assigned its proportionate share of the total number of graduate assistantships and fellowships available within the institution.

(2) Part-time work opportunities appropriate for students in the program are identified and efforts are made to secure assignments for those desiring such assistance.

(3) Loan resources are made available to students in counselor education.

(4) Prospective students are provided information about possible sources of financial assistance.

b. Personal counseling services are available to all counselor candidates.

(1) Available counselors are identified.

(2) This service is available from staff members other than the members of the counselor education staff.

(3) Patterns for referral are known to all staff members and are communicated to all students.

Index of Names

Index of Subjects

THE BOOK MANUFACTURE

Counseling in the Elementary School was typeset and offset printed by Webb Publishing Company. Binding was by A. J. Dahl Co. The paper is Perkins & Squire Company's Glatfelter Old Forge. Internal and cover design was by John Goetz. The type in this book is Baskerville with Bodoni Modern Roman headings.